CONQUER YOUR FUTURE

CONQUER
YOUR
FUTURE

Unlocking the Secret
to Business and Life Mastery

HUBERT HUMPHREY

Forefront
BOOKS

Published by Forefront Books, Nashville, Tennessee.

Distributed by Simon & Schuster.

Scripture quotations are taken from the Holy Bible,
King James Version (1604). Public domain.

Library of Congress Control Number: 2025900989

Print ISBN: 9781637633359
E-book ISBN: 9781637633366

Cover Design by George Stevens, G Sharp Design LLC
Interior Design by by Bill Kersey, KerseyGraphics

Printed in the United States of America

*This book is lovingly dedicated to my eternal companion,
Norma, and our four incredible children: Jody, Kim, Jeffrey,
and Jennifer. Their unwavering support through the years
has been the foundation of my success. Without them, all
the achievements in the world would hold no meaning.*

*Also to all of the amazing teammates, mentors, and leaders
over the years who have contributed to my life and success.*

TABLE OF CONTENTS

PART TWO
THE FIRST GREAT CONQUEST OF THE ODYSSEY:
THE A.L. WILLIAMS COMPANY (ALW) ERA

*Every person who has ever been born on this earth desires more.
The word "enthusiasm" comes from the Greek word* entheos,
which means "God within." Everyone has entheos. *All we have
to do is activate the power that's embedded in them.*

*"For ordinary people to do extraordinary things, a system—
'a way of doing things'—is absolutely essential in order to compensate
for the disparity between the skills your people have and the skills your
business needs if it is to produce consistent results." —The E-Myth*

*The System Begins with a Recruiter's Mentality. It doesn't start with a sales
mentality. Recruiting is an all-the-time thing. It is a state of mind.*

*You can't just recruit someone and expect them to become a leader all by themselves.
You have to guide them through the System's Six Steps and Eight Speed Filters.*

*I knew that my team would only rise to the level of their vision.
So, I needed to send them to exciting events and put them in front of
leaders who could stretch their vision in ways I couldn't do alone.*

*Every human being is hardwired to want to be recognized, rewarded, noticed,
and emotionally fed. They want to be significant and know they matter.*

*Having a system makes things predictable, foolproof, and profitable,
so I built a duplicatable system where a new recruit's chances for success are very high.*

PART THREE
THE SECOND GREAT CONQUEST OF THE ODYSSEY:
WORLD MARKETING ALLIANCE (WMA)

IT ONLY TAKES A SPARK

HAVE YOU EVER HAD A VISION FOR YOUR FUTURE THAT WAS SO powerful you could hardly wait to get there? But that vision seemed so far away you didn't know how to reach it? Well, as the Founder and CEO of Hegemon Group International (HGI), one of the fastest-growing companies in the financial services industry, I am here to tell you that I found a way to arrive at that future.

I sometimes jokingly say that I got to my dream future by train, but that's only partly true. I actually learned and mastered a secret so powerful that I feel obligated to share it with the world. That secret advanced my success and the success of those who joined me. What has happened since then is the stuff of legends. Let me explain.

Throughout a seventeen-year career working as a railroad conductor, I constantly tried many entrepreneurial ventures —mostly side opportunities—desperately hoping to escape what was, at the time, a very grueling and dangerous line of work. Fueled by a voracious desire to gain financial freedom, I kept my *Trying Motor* going until the circumstances were right for me to strike. Then strike I did with a revolutionary dream-selling, team-building system. Through drive and perseverance, I successfully made the leap, as I like to say, "from boxcar to business star."

Today, after pioneering and building three great multi-billion-dollar businesses and becoming a member of the Entrepreneurship Hall of Fame, my mission of creating wealth for families remains the same, though the width and breadth of that mission has certainly increased. I've always known that my success is tied to the success of all of the many thousands of *Driven, Determined Dreamers* who have followed me. I couldn't have conquered my future without helping people, like you, to conquer their future. Not only have I talked the talk, I have walked the walk. The words in this book aren't just neat self-help anecdotes; they are methods I have actually practiced—things I've actually done. Since that gives me some *moral authority* on the subject, I feel I also have a *moral responsibility* to tell you how to succeed too. Through this book, I am sharing my secrets with *everyone* who wants to know.

Why now?

The circumstances are ripe. People are quitting their jobs in record numbers. Starting their own businesses. Changing careers and professions. Looking for more control over their destinies. With the changes in technology, they are searching the internet for two main things—a *financial education* (they want to know how money works) and a *business education* (they want to know how to start a business of their own).

I recall that time in my own life well. I started out as a flagman riding an actual red caboose in the Southeastern Division of the Central Georgia Railroad. I wore heavy work boots, dusty jeans, and a railroad cap, and I carried a railroad lantern in my hand as I traveled long stretches of track. It was a hard life during which I survived collisions, was thrown from and nearly run over by a moving train, was struck by lightning, and even endured the job-related death of a dear childhood friend while he was substituting for me on a trip. All the while, I refused to give up on my dream of "being somebody special." My journey—from riding a caboose to disrupting and reshaping one of the largest industries in the world—led to changing the life-insurance buying habits and savings habits of Middle America as a whole.

In this book, I will discuss how I've used my proven and tested system (hereinafter referred to as *the System*) to help millions of new entrepreneurs turn their dreams into reality and create wealth for themselves and their families.

Through my own example and through the success stories of the individuals I've mentored, you will learn how to *conquer your future* too. As you follow the System's principles, which I clearly lay out for you, your future will become more predictable, foolproof, and profitable.

So, wherever you are in your career journey—whether you are still searching, are at the beginning of a new venture, or you've stalled out—I'm confident the secrets in this book can meet you where you are and help you not only get back on track but get you to where you were always meant to be.

Remember, *it only takes a small spark to ignite a great future.*

PART ONE

AMWAY AND THE RAILROAD

CHAPTER 1

HUMBLE BEGINNINGS

YOU CAN'T TRULY UNDERSTAND A PERSON UNTIL YOU'VE LEARNED about their family. So, before we start this journey together, let me tell you briefly about mine. I was born in Macon, Georgia, as the first child of Steeley Hubert Humphrey Sr. and June Humphrey. My mother was very petite, weighing less than a hundred pounds when I was born. I, on the other hand, came into the world weighing ten pounds! That's about a tenth of my mother's weight. What an entrance I made! A few months later, my mother registered me in a baby pageant where I won a year's worth of free baby food, diaper service, and a $25 savings bond. You could say that I started paying my way in life immediately. Yep, I was destined for big things.

As a child, I attended Cynthia Weir Elementary School, the same school all of my children would eventually attend. I was an excellent student and enjoyed academics. I even won the Bibb County Spelling Bee when I was in the seventh grade. My parents went on to have two girls, Sandra and Maria, and another boy, Cleon. Later, my father and his second wife, Margaret, had my youngest brother, Steve. They have all played a great role in my life, providing me with love and friendship.

My mother was the youngest of ten children. She developed rheumatic fever as a child, which would negatively affect her life when she became an adult. She was a small, beautiful woman who never had much of a childhood because she was so ill while growing up and was quite young when she married my father, who was six years older than her. Then, just one year after their wedding, I was born. Before she knew it, three more children came along and suddenly she was a mother of four. The rheumatic fever she'd had as a child developed into rheumatoid arthritis. This was a devastating and painful affliction that, over time, crippled her completely and eventually took her life.

I don't recall my mother ever having much time for herself. She always prioritized taking care of her four children. Once she became ill, my father didn't quite know how to handle it. He was a good man, but he didn't have the empathy and patience she needed, and he never really understood the magnitude of her illness. My mother and father loved each other, but because my mother had married so young, was so sick as a child, and was now becoming sick as an adult, she longed to enjoy some of the freedom she'd missed out on earlier. She decided she wanted out of the marriage. My father tried to convince her to stay, but once he saw how determined she was to leave, they divorced. This crushed my father, and he was never quite the same. I was seventeen years old when they divorced.

During my teenage and young adult years, my father was busy with his career, which, ironically, was in the insurance business. He won all of the contests, awards, and trips and was successful in his world. But that success wouldn't last long. His company, Colonial Life, was sold, and instead of letting my father and others remain independent agents, the new company wanted to turn them into "captive agents" (agents who only work for one insurance company). When my father fought against this, because he believed it would limit his potential, the company took his accounts and assigned them to company agents. This left him without renewals and with a dwindling income.

My father wasn't financially prepared for such a turn of events. He stayed with the company for a time, all the while becoming more bitter, discouraged, and depressed. This blow, on top of his divorce a few years earlier, turned him from a fun-loving man with a wonderful personality into someone who was depressed and held grudges for the rest of his life. He got married a couple more times but could never let go of the past.

Sadly, once my mother's condition became more chronic, she had a change of heart and regretted getting a divorce. She probably would have welcomed the chance to be with my father again, but he could not handle her advanced illness.

Unfortunately, the major lesson I learned from my dad was what *not* to do in the face of adversity. I saw what he went through and decided to take control of my destiny. I refused to become someone who just reacted to things or let others dictate my life.

CHAPTER 2

BORN A DRIVEN,
DETERMINED DREAMER

GROWING UP IN MACON, GEORGIA, DURING THE 1950S WAS A blessing. Rock and roll was just blossoming, and Macon was a hot spot in the music world. Elvis Presley, Chuck Berry, Buddy Holly, and others were bursting onto the national scene with this incredible new sound, and I was hooked. Our local claim to fame was Richard Wayne Penniman, who later became known as Little Richard. Before he rose to fame, he was a dishwasher on weekdays at the local bus stop and a singing carhop on weekends at the Pig 'N Whistle barbecue joint, where we would go listen to him sing and perform.

One day Little Richard was nowhere to be found. None of us knew where he'd gone. But then, I'll never forget the moment when I figured it out. I came home from school, turned the radio to WIBB—the local rhythm and blues station—and heard the DJ, King Bee, excitedly announce, "We found him! We found him! He's been gone, but we found him! Here's Macon's own Little Richard. He signed a contract with Specialty Records. Listen to this new hit. Hold on to your hat." Then he played the song "Tutti Frutti." I had never heard anything like those first words blasting across the airwaves: *"Wop bop a loo bop a lop bom bom."* After that, I just knew I had to become a rock star somehow.

When I was fifteen, my best friend's sister was dating a true-to-life rock 'n' roll star with a couple of big hits. When his tour came through Macon, she talked him into letting us go with him on his tour bus. So, without telling my mom, we hopped on the bus and for two days traveled with them through the Carolinas. As we watched the group up close, we learned what it felt like to perform in front of so many cheering fans.

The energy of this era made a huge impression on me that has lasted a lifetime. I desperately wanted to *be somebody*. I wanted to be up there on a stage and be a star. It didn't exactly happen in the music world, as I had hoped and planned, mostly because I possessed no talent for singing or playing an instrument. But I did ultimately find success building great marketing teams in the financial services world, and I would often stand on stages in front of thousands of excited entrepreneurs, many of whom wanted to be mentored by me.

I definitely went through my phases in life, including a *Rebel Without a Cause* period where I sported a pompadour hairstyle and a leather jacket. I was the original Fonzi long before *Happy Days*—chasing girls and getting into trouble.

After high school, I attended Georgia Tech, preparing for a career in the real world. I imagined graduating with a job in a big company that offered a nice salary, good benefits, and a solid retirement package. I was the first person in my family to attend college. Everything was going smoothly. I was an excellent student and even made the dean's list. But one of the many glorious accidents that happened throughout my life was about to unfold.

The summer following my first year at Georgia Tech, I married my sweetheart, Norma Patrick. During my sophomore year, we learned we were going to have our first child. With a baby on the way, I knew I needed to earn money, so when the school year ended, I looked for some summer work. My best friend, Larry Hinson, who had just started a job on the railroad two months earlier, showed me his paycheck and that got me excited. I applied to work there too, and, unexpectedly, they hired me. Little did I know that this so-called summer job would end my college career and begin a seventeen-year stint with the railroad that felt more like a life sentence.

Everyone is going to face challenges and obstacles at some point. The most successful people learn how to turn those challenges into opportunities. Unfortunately, most don't choose the right path in those circumstances. They take the path of least resistance and follow the safety of the crowd. The typically more successful route is best explained by one of my favorite quotes from Robert Frost: "Two roads diverged in a wood, and I—I took the one less traveled by, and that has made all the difference."[1]

CHAPTER 3

MY FIRST EPIPHANY:
WHO PUT ME ON THIS TRAIN?!

As a small boy, I loved going to the movies and always dreamt about becoming one of the heroes I saw on the silver screen. But I wasn't content to just dream. As someone who was never afraid of work, I was always doing something to make money. I had a newspaper route. I was a soda jerk. I was a grocery delivery boy. I worked in my uncle's heavy-machinery repair shop. I sold women's shoes. I worked at a bakery—though, after only four days on the midnight shift, standing beside the 130-degree oven, I quit. In fact, I resisted eating their bread for years afterward. I was a plumbing assistant at Callaway Plumbing. I worked in HVAC with my cousin, crawling under houses and wrapping ductwork with insulation. I tarred super-hot roofs. I held a job at the Jones and Grissom Printing Company, helping with cleanup and delivery. These are just a few of the many jobs I tried before finally going off to Georgia Tech to pursue a college degree, only to end up working on the railroad.

During my early years of train work, I told myself that everything would be okay because I was making a better-than-average income for someone who had never graduated college. I had joined the union, too, so I would be protected. But then as the bills started to mount, the children were born, and there were hungry mouths to feed, I really felt the pressure. Finally, it dawned on me that I was a full-fledged, card-carrying adult and life was kickin' my butt. One day, while just going about my mundane business as a railroad man, riding on the caboose during one of my many trips from Macon to Columbus, I had an epiphany. It was as if I had awakened from a coma. I realized I had fallen into a kind of sleepwalking existence. I had become a passive observer who was now stuck in an endless loop. Instead of living, I was simply letting things happen to me. But, for some reason, on that day, under the weight of a life I had not planned, I stopped and took a hard look at myself. There I was, in worn workman's boots and clothes, sitting on a dusty caboose with my lantern in my hand. I remember saying to myself, *Stop this train! Who put me on this train? Let me off!* Suddenly, I had a vision of a lonely old railroad conductor needing help getting onto the caboose. When I looked into his face, I was totally shocked to see it was ME! It made me realize that I had chosen the wrong path. My future looked very bleak. I had to find some way to escape this runaway train I was on—and fast.

I awoke from that day's vision with a vengeance and vowed from that moment onward I would do everything I could to get out of the railroad life, no matter how long it took. No more sleepwalking through life! I was determined to *be somebody*. I wanted to control my own future—take hold of my destiny. *I wanted financial freedom.* I didn't know exactly how to make that happen, but I started trying, and I was filled with the determination to make it happen. I had seen what financial pressures had done to my father, his career, and his marriage, and I wasn't going to let that happen to me. Little did I know that it would take thirteen more years to gain my freedom, during which time I would endure numerous near-death experiences on the job. But the sleeping giant had been awakened and there was no turning back. I was like the fabled character Rip Van Winkle, who fell asleep for twenty years. When he went to sleep, King George of England was his ruler, and when he awakened George Washington was his president. In those twenty years, he had missed the entire Revolutionary War.[2]

I started looking for new opportunities. I wanted to get off the track I was on—literally. I looked at a few different businesses, but I preferred to start one of my own. The more I investigated that prospect, the more I saw it wasn't all fun and games. There was pressure and money required. I wasn't going to get a better job than the one I had, so my options were limited. At one point, I heard about a company called Continental Marketing (a forerunner to membership-only buying clubs). There was a low cost to join, but it never panned out. Next, I was invited to a meeting at the Dempsey Hotel in Macon to learn more about an opportunity with a company called Koskot. They marketed women's cosmetics made with mink oil. This turned out to be a pyramid scheme and I knew I wasn't going to get involved in that, so I left the meeting. As I was exiting the building, I ran into a friend who had walked out as well. He called the next day and came by to show me information on Amway. This was the first time I'd heard about multiples and overrides (opportunities to earn commissions on downline sales in addition to commissions on personal sales). I was interested but remained open to other opportunities too.

A year later, the Koskot company was shut down. Glen Turner, who was with them, started the Dare to Be Great business—another pyramid company. I didn't join that either. My cousin Lee Jones called me about a meeting for Holiday Magic. He'd previewed a video about it in his basement. It was also a pyramid. I passed on that opportunity too, and I'm glad I did. Twenty years later, while visiting Lee's old house, I went down to the basement and was amazed to find stacks of unsold inventory from that company still lying there under a plastic covering. I saw firsthand how inventory-loading schemes worked. They just filled up people's homes and garages with goods. My instincts all those years prior had guided me well. I had thankfully avoided other tempting businesses like these and settled into the low start-up cost and unlimited earning potential of Amway.

I gave Amway a try part-time—for eight years. Although that wasn't where I ultimately found success, that simple decision, made from a determination to wake up and do something more with my life, would shape my future in ways I never could have imagined. What saved me was the fact that I remained a Driven, Determined Dreamer.

Are you sleepwalking through life? If so, wake up and take control of your destiny!

CHAPTER 4

NEVER QUIT DREAMING

WHEN I BEGAN WORKING WITH AMWAY, THE COMPANY WAS STILL in its early days. It was a simple, grassroots opportunity that offered great possibilities and, luckily for me, didn't require start-up money. There I learned about the magic of multiples. By recruiting people who recruited others, I saw myself building a big team that could potentially make all of us lots of money. I fell in love with Amway's system and vision. They were part of a whole new exciting industry that was emerging called *multi-level marketing*.

I started my eight-year journey with Amway by working part-time, hoping that it might eventually lead to my escape from the railroad. I so desperately wanted out of my full-time job that my passionate pursuit of this elusive Amway dream nearly cost me half of my railroad time and thus half of my regular income. Even though I was working the business as hard as I could, I was making very little money. But I was hooked. The concept made sense to me, and I'm still infected with the multiplication mentality to this day. These early lessons set the foundation for everything that was about to come. And in the long run, the investment of my time and energy, along with the lessons learned during this time, helped me to build future great companies that created wealth for me and thousands of others.

CHAPTER 5

TAKE ADVANTAGE OF LIFE'S GLORIOUS ACCIDENTS

LIFE IS FULL OF UNPLANNED MOMENTS THAT, IF RECOGNIZED, offer unlimited possibilities. I call these moments "glorious accidents." What matters is what we do with them. My working at Amway while trying to escape the railroad was one such moment. It didn't bring in much livable cash flow, as I said, but my time there taught me things that would later result in millions of dollars of income, provide wealth for thousands of families, and lead me to build three multibillion-dollar market cap companies in the financial services industry. And all that happened because of another glorious accident.

It was 1975, and I was grinding away on the railroad and Amway simultaneously. I had actually built a small team, but all I had to show for my efforts was a house full of soaps and detergents and a frustrated wife. One day, I received a note on the Campbell Worldwide Diamond Association letterhead. It was from Bill Campbell, the first person in Amway to achieve Triple Diamond—level status.

I knew Bill, but not too well, and I definitely wasn't doing enough production to be a part of any Diamond Association. He was my upline, but he was *way up* the line. It turns out the letter was meant for Diamond Club members only, and the fact that I got it was completely by accident. However, that didn't stop me from opening it or hoping to find some kind of secret to Amway success.

The letter itself was only one page with a few words written on it. The heading said, "The Start," and then these six points were listed:

Prospect

Contact

Meeting

Follow-up

Start-up

Duplication

If this was the secret to success, then it was safe with me. I had no idea what any of it meant. I thought, *Is this a code for something?*

I called Bill's office and explained who I was. No surprise, his secretary had never heard of me. I was a little fish far down the line. Still, I persisted, explaining that I had received the letter and wanted to know if he'd left something out or if there was a set of instructions to go with it.

The secretary sounded surprised (perhaps even horrified) that I had the letter because it was only for the big dogs. "Oh no," she said, "you weren't supposed to get that! It was only meant for the Diamond Club!" Having been the person likely responsible for the mistake, she was probably as concerned about losing her job as anything else. That just clued me in to the fact that there was something special about the accidental letter. I didn't know what it was exactly, but I knew enough about Bill to know that if he'd sent it out, then it had meaning. Bill was an engineer by trade and loved to simplify things, paring them down to the bare necessities for his team. If you've ever heard me say you need to "simplify to multiply," you have Bill Campbell to thank. That was his line, and I have since borrowed it and made it my own.

I went back and studied the letter. That exercise appealed to my Georgia Tech engineering mind as well. I liked simple steps that I could follow and then repeat. And while I didn't have a business background or know how to start a business, I could follow simple instructions. No further explanation came from Bill's office about the letter, so it was left to me to interpret it. I studied each step intently.

"What does *prospecting* mean?" I wondered aloud. "What does *contacting* mean?" Then I saw the sequence of it. "A prospect is no good if I never contact them, so what am I contacting them about?"

I realized it was to invite them to an *Opportunity Meeting*. Bill had always talked about recruiting people, so it seemed reasonable to me that he invited people to attend the meeting instead of selling them on the product. This made sense, because I had realized by then that I would never make a living by just selling soap. Okay, so I needed to start recruiting. Then I continued through the rest of the steps, talking my way through them until I thought I had figured them all out. It was so simple, yet so effective.

I began playing around with this new System and soon started to resurrect my struggling Amway business. In about a year, I had roughly a thousand people on my team. I still wasn't making much money, but I was having fun seeing the possibilities of the new, simple System that resulted from the glorious accident. Using the System, I recruited leaders who would follow me. This was a revelation. I learned that recruiting wasn't the end of the game. Recruiting was just getting the raw material. Following these simple steps helped me to finally build a promising team, but it still hadn't translated into big cash flow.

This was the genesis of my *Leadership Format System (LFS)* that led to the building of three great companies in the financial services world. This glorious accident wasn't as simple as winning the lottery—I had to take what had happened, puzzle it out, and then give it a go, learning through trial and error. The lesson here is that you must stay prepared and motivated so you can recognize and take advantage of such defining, life-changing moments when they occur.

CHAPTER 6

DREAM FUEL FOR YOUR
OWN FIREBOX

AN IMPORTANT FACT I LEARNED FROM SOME OF THE VETERAN railroad men who came before me proved to be very valuable in my life. I learned that human beings work the same way as old steam engines did. An old steam engine's firebox had to reach 212 degrees to produce the steam required to move. Getting to that level was one person's primary responsibility: the fireman. The fireman worked hard and strategically to shovel just enough coal to reach that critical temperature. He would carefully bank the coal to avoid snuffing out the fire and to steadily raise the temperature to 212 degrees. He had to do this as fast as he could. Then, he had to maintain that level. If the heat in the firebox dropped below 212 degrees, the water would cease converting into steam and the engine could no longer pull the train.

All of us have an internal firebox as well. Our job is to tend it, stoking the fires of our drive and determination. But that doesn't mean we should go all out, mindlessly shoveling hard and fast. It might seem like a sure way to get moving, but that approach can easily cause us to burn out. Chances are you've experienced this before or seen it in others. Instead, you should act as the skilled fireman of your own firebox. Learn what it takes to keep the temperature—*your motivation*—consistently above the 212-degree mark. It will help you keep your career and life swiftly moving along the tracks. If you drop your motivation level below 212 degrees, you greatly decrease your chances of success.

CHAPTER 7

STRUCK BY LIGHTNING
(LITERALLY!)

ONE COLD AND STORMY NIGHT WHEN I WAS ABOUT TWENTY-FIVE years old, I was on my shift as a flagman on the caboose of Southwest 136, returning to Macon from Columbus in the middle of what we called the "Dark Territory." It was named that because it was on a portion of the railroad that had not been wired for electronic communication signals. We had been instructed to make an unplanned stop to pick up some train cars at the Howard Sand Pit.

Any time our long freight train made a stop in this dark territory, we had to be very careful not to be rear-ended by an oncoming train, and that's where I came in. As the flagman, I strapped on the thirty-pound radio, grabbed my supplies and flashlight, and walked about two miles down the tracks from our train in the dark to put exploding caps on the rails. When an oncoming train ran over those caps, the explosion would create a loud warning sound notifying the conductor to stop ASAP because there was another train on the tracks just ahead. These trains were pulling ten thousand tons at sixty miles per hour and usually needed more than a mile and a half to come to a safe stop.

After I placed the caps and headed back to my train, I heard my train's horn blow the signal for the flagman to get back in, which meant they were leaving in ten minutes. I tried radioing them to let them know I wasn't on the train yet, but my old radio had shorted out in the rain, and I couldn't communicate with anyone. I was already walking as fast as I could because running on wet railroad ties and gravel in the dark is nearly impossible. Since the train was so long and had so much slack bunched up, I hoped it would take a while for the slack to run out and the whole train to get going. I was huffing and puffing and praying I'd make it.

When I was close to a hundred yards away, I heard the rattling of the train cars; all the slack had run out, and the train started moving. I increased my pace. I was about fifty yards away by then and the train was picking up speed. I sprinted with all I had and got within twenty-five yards . . . then ten . . . then . . . I wasn't getting any closer, so I gave it one last try, but my legs finally gave out. I fell on the wet tracks and then rolled into a ditch, landing in a heap. I lay there, my chest heaving, staring up into the Dark Territory's night sky, trying to figure out what to do.

The situation wasn't good. Not only was I in the Dark Territory with a dead radio, but I was roughly sixty miles from any civilization. It was cold and storming, and I was soaked and chilled to the bone. I prayed that the other train would finally come by so I could flag them down. Otherwise, I was in for a very long night.

After pulling myself together, I made my way to a nearby railroad telephone box that had a big metal covering with an old crank phone beneath it. Thankfully, it worked. I called and explained the situation to the chief dispatcher. He told me the train that was supposed to be coming was having engine issues and that another wouldn't be by for four or five hours! There was nothing to do but sit, wait, and freeze until that train came. I figured at least things couldn't be any worse. Boy, was I wrong.

I soon realized that standing, dripping wet, under a metal roof during a lightning storm wasn't the best idea. Right then, a bolt of lightning struck the pole, blasting me fifteen or twenty feet away from the phone, knocking me out. When I awoke, I didn't know what had happened or how long I had been unconscious, but my head was pounding, my ears were ringing, and my right arm (the one that had been holding the phone to my ear) felt as if it was on fire. I did an inventory of my body parts and found that everything was intact. All I could do was just lie there in the rain, mud, and sand. After a while, when my hearing started to return, I stumbled back to the phone. When I picked it up and found that it still worked, I couldn't help but chuckle and think to myself, *I was just nearly blown to bits, but nothing happened to this old phone!* I contacted the dispatcher again, letting him know what had happened and asking him to send the train to get me.

It took about two hours before I could use my arm again and another two hours for the train to finally come and rescue me. How I had survived was a miracle. They gave me some dry clothes and put me on the second engine to rest and get warm. Then, in typical railroad fashion, that was the end of the story. No doctor. No checkup. They just sent me home and told me when to come back for my next shift. I later found out what had saved me: My arm was bent while I was holding the phone to my ear, so the electrical charge was able to exit through my elbow.

You will likely go through your entire life without getting struck by lightning, but you might survive another kind of near-death encounter that could have easily gone the other way. Should that happen, there's no doubt you'll suffer setbacks and injuries. The important thing, however, is to let it make you stronger. Of course, the impact of trying and failing at a business venture is miniscule in comparison to such life-threatening events. Even so, find a business with a System that makes the risk of failure as remote as the odds of getting struck by lightning.

CHAPTER 8

"HUBERT'S BEEN KILLED!"

IF YOU THINK THAT LIGHTNING STORY WAS INCREDIBLE, YOU'VE got to hear about this next experience that happened a few years later. Of all of the defining moments in my life, this one has to be at the top. I was scheduled to work as the conductor on a shift, but there was an Amway meeting I didn't want to miss. I called the crew dispatcher to request the night off. He said they were swamped and had no relief personnel available. I was disappointed, but I started to get ready for my trip that night. A short time later, the crew dispatcher called back and said that he had overlooked a note from my friend Larry Hinson saying he was requesting time off later in the week and that he'd be willing to switch trips with me. This was great news. So I put on my sport coat and went to my Amway meeting instead of my shift on the railroad. I was so excited about building this new business that was going to help me attain the financial freedom I so desperately wanted.

After the meeting, I came home like every other evening and went to sleep. In the middle of the night our phone rang. Calls that late are rarely good news. Still half asleep, Norma answered it to hear, "Mrs. Humphrey, I'm sorry to tell you that there was a head-on collision involving your husband's train, and he was killed." Norma sat up in bed, now fully awake, processing what she had just heard. Next, she turned to make sure I was lying beside her.

"Hubert is right here next to me," she told the man, who was now just as confused as she was. If it wasn't Hubert, then who was it? It turns out that only one of the ten crew members on those two trains had been killed. Sadly, it was Larry Hinson, who was filling in for me as the conductor that night. The man on the phone didn't realize that we had swapped positions.

Larry had been my best friend since we were kids. He had been the best man at my wedding and the one who sold me on the idea of working on the railroad in the first place. But as fate would have it, I was off trying to find a better life for my family that evening. My entrepreneurial ambition literally saved my life.

As word of the collision and the death of the conductor spread, everyone assumed it had been me. Even Norma's father, who also worked on the railroad, thought it was me. When he heard the news announced on the train radio, he passed out cold.

I think about that fateful night often. Looking back today, I see, even more clearly, God's hand. I feel strongly that it was God's plan. He needed Larry on the other side early, and He needed me to stay a little longer on this earth to accomplish some unfinished, very important work. I vowed, from that day forward, to do my best to make the most of every day—to make something out of myself and help others to do the same. I knew, right then, that I couldn't depend on any more luck in my life, because it certainly seemed it was all used up on that one night.

Don't take a single day for granted. Go out and live every day as if it was your last.

CHAPTER 9

ALWAYS KEEP YOUR
TRYING MOTOR RUNNING

WHILE I WAS STRUGGLING TO GROW MY AMWAY BUSINESS IN THE early years, my cash flow wasn't keeping up. Our little eleven-hundred-square-foot house was now packed with our four children. Luckily, I persisted at doing the one thing I was good at—keeping my Trying Motor running. I had faith that one day I would find the right escape vehicle. In addition to the railroad and Amway, my days were filled with providing for Norma and the kids, and taking care of my mother, making sure her last days were as comfortable as possible.

My mother was such an inspiration to me. In spite of all the obstacles she faced, she never gave up. She had endured poor health most of her life, from her youth onward. She died too early, at age fifty-one, from the effects of rheumatoid arthritis. After watching her go through her refiner's fire and still remain positive, the inscription I chose for her gravestone says it all: "*She lived with dignity, She suffered with dignity, She died with dignity.*"

This was a low point for me. Life had seemed to pile on, and I was feeling beaten down. I had given up half of my railroad income trying to grow my Amway business, but I was never able to make it profitable. I was spending fifty to sixty hours a week on the railroad, twenty-five hours a week on Amway, and serving an additional thirty hours a week as Bishop—an unpaid, volunteer, lay-ministry position in our church. I had dug myself a deep hole of debt and bills. No matter what I tried, it appeared I couldn't shovel my way out. I didn't know it then, but I had violated what I later learned to be the *Law of Holes,* which states that when you find yourself in a hole, you should QUIT DIGGING!

I had a little desk in my office at home with a big pile of bills on it. One day, I just pulled the desk out, lifted it up, and let everything on top slide behind it. I said, "If they want the money badly enough, they know where to find me." The bills were mounting faster than I knew what to do about them—and then, on December 29, 1977, my mother passed away. I even pushed my wonderful life partner, Norma, to the brink. She was wanting to escape all of this stress too. She almost persuaded me to give up my dream of being an entrepreneur and just live the life of a full-time railroad man. She had me nearly convinced. My arms were three quarters of the way up to surrender. But, at the last second, I snatched them back down and told her that I would rather she take a gun and shoot me before I'd surrender to the railroad. I would always tease her, saying that I was glad we didn't have a gun or any bullets in the house.

PART TWO

THE FIRST
GREAT CONQUEST
OF THE ODYSSEY:
THE A.L. WILLIAMS
COMPANY (ALW) ERA

CHAPTER 10

IT ONLY TAKES A SMALL SPARK
TO IGNITE A GREAT FUTURE

THE DAY AFTER MY MOTHER'S FUNERAL, I GOT A CALL FROM A church acquaintance and mentor, Ronnie Graybeal Sr., who told me that his son, Ronnie Jr., had gotten involved in something and wanted to come see me about it.

At the time, I was the Bishop (very much like a pastor, except, as I mentioned, it was a lay volunteer role) of our local congregation. Ronnie Jr. was married and had a young family, but he had been inactive in the church for several years. His dad didn't know why Ronnie Jr. wanted to see Bishop Humphrey and was just hopeful that a visit with me might help lead him back into church activity. Since I was a *shepherd*, metaphorically speaking, anytime a *lost sheep* wanted to visit, I welcomed it.

When Ronnie Jr. came over, he started talking about an insurance concept he had stumbled across. Now, this was not the conversation I was expecting to have. He was probably the last person on earth I thought would come talk to me about insurance—or business in general. He had spent much of his time in a band playing in bars, and now he was here to speak with his spiritual counselor *about insurance*? I often wonder what would have happened had I not been available. This unexpected visit from a most unlikely messenger proved to be one of the most profound turning points of my life.

I watched as Ronnie Jr. scratched out on a legal pad a new insurance concept called *Buy Term and Invest the Difference*. His presentation was raw, but the underlying logic made sense and intrigued me. What interested me more, though, was the fact that he had made over $5,000 during his first month in this brand-new company called A.L. Williams (ALW), which was founded by a former high school football coach named Arthur L. ("Art") Williams.

Even though Ronnie Jr. couldn't answer most of my questions with more than the words "I don't know," what little he told me was enough to get my attention. What he had was something I call *Ignorant Enthusiasm*, which I learned a long time ago is one of the most powerful commodities that a leader in our business needs to have. Ronnie Jr. unknowingly did all of the right things to activate both my *Curiosity Button* and my *Greed Button*. I have spent a lifetime trying to teach people to *purposely* do to their recruit prospects what he accidentally did to me.

I knew that if he could make that kind of money, I sure as heck could. I went down to see Ronnie Jr.'s manager, Jack Schulman, to have my main question answered: "How did Ronnie Jr. make so much money so fast?" Jack showed me two phenomenal, industry-changing and life-altering paradigms. The first was the full power of the Buy Term and Invest the Difference concept to replace outdated, cash value, whole life policies. And the second was the tremendous income potential that the annualization of premiums for a 75 percent advance of annual commissions on submission of an application with a simple check for just the first month's premium (usually $50 per month with a voided check) could yield.

All of a sudden, it clicked in my mind. By taking what I had learned about the secret to recruiting and building a system from my Amway years, and coupling that knowledge with what I'd just learned on the first day I signed up with ALW, I realized

I had just found the vehicle that would help me finally escape the railroad. I could see that this magical combination of multiples and money products was the key to building an Amway of insurance and investments.

What I also found was an idea whose time had come. At that moment I felt just like Ray Kroc when he first met the McDonald brothers at their San Bernardino, California, location while he was trying to sell them a new milkshake mixer. As he waited to speak to the brothers, he observed their operation and caught a vision of how to franchise their system throughout the country. After talking with them, he realized that they didn't know how big this could be. Similarly, I quickly realized that while the ALW managers had a great product and a crusading message, they did not have the systems knowledge to build a giant distribution team. But *I DID!*

I was incredibly prepared for this opportunity. My desire was white-hot, and I was willing to do whatever was required of me to succeed. To know exactly how badly I wanted this to work, read one of my favorite stories below and whenever you see the word *wisdom*, substitute for it the word *success*.

A rich young man came to Socrates in search of wisdom. He walked up to him and said, "O great Socrates, I come to you for wisdom." Socrates, recognizing a pompous fool when he saw one, led him down to the sea and took him chest deep into the water. Then he asked him, "What did you say you wanted?" "Wisdom, O great Socrates," said the young man.

Socrates put his strong hands on the man's shoulders and pushed him under. Thirty seconds later Socrates let him up. "What do you want?" he asked again. "Wisdom," the young man sputtered, "O great and wise Socrates." Socrates pushed him under again. Thirty seconds, thirty-five, forty—then Socrates let him up. The man was gasping. "What do you want, young man?"

Between heavy breaths the fellow wheezed, "Wisdom! O wise and wonderful..." Socrates jammed him under again—forty seconds passed, then fifty, then he let him up.

"What do you want?" "AIR!" the young man yelled. "I NEED AIR!"

When you want wisdom as much as you have just wanted air, then you will find it!"[3]

Much like that young man, I had been pursuing but never achieving success because I hadn't yet raised my desire level to the 212-degree mark I spoke of earlier. Up until this point, I had only been wishing and hoping. I had not yet mastered the art of stretching my vision to fuel my desire.

Rarely does an opportunity knock on your door and introduce itself as the opportunity you've been looking for. Most of the time it's hidden—and can come from even the most unlikely of sources. Unless you're really looking, there is a good chance you won't see it.

In later chapters, you will more fully understand the magnitude of this historic window of opportunity I was so blessed to be a part of.

CHAPTER 11

INTRODUCING ART WILLIAMS

I THINK IT'S IMPORTANT FOR YOU TO UNDERSTAND WHERE ART'S passion and crusade came from. When Art was in his early twenties, his father suddenly died of a heart attack. His family had been sold whole life insurance that left them woefully underinsured, putting an unnecessary strain on his mother to raise and provide for their growing family. This really upset Art, and he never forgave the insurance industry. In fact, that's why he declared war on the industry. Many years later, when Art was coaching football at a new high school in Columbus, Georgia, his cousin, who was a CPA, introduced him to the concept of Buy Term and Invest the Difference. He then realized how much of a difference this would have made to his family. It fueled Art's mission to change the way the life insurance industry served middle-income America.

Art started working part-time selling this new concept to family and friends. Shortly thereafter, he left coaching and moved to Atlanta to pursue this new career full-time. He spent about four years with a couple of companies learning to develop a team. Before he founded ALW, he was with a more traditional agency called Waddell and Reed. Art was recruiting greenies (new people to the insurance field), and even then, he was riling up the troops to beat Prudential and shake up the industry. But Waddell and Reed wasn't on the same page. They weren't too excited about taking on that Goliath. They were more content to just keep the status quo.

Inspired by his hero, legendary Alabama football coach Bear Bryant, Art too wanted to be a championship coach. He knew that if he was ever going to win the equivalent of a national championship in the life insurance business, he would have to beat Prudential. Art often said that he felt like "Moby Dick in a goldfish bowl" because Waddell and Reed didn't share this same dream. So, he left them to start his own company with about fifty of his agents. They named it A.L. Williams (ALW). By the time I joined, there were about thirty active agents producing business.

Very few people have had more of an impact on my life than Art Williams—and he will certainly be in the pantheon of all-time great business leaders in financial services history.

For sure, one of the similarities Art and I shared is that we are both blessed with tremendous spouses. I have Norma, and he has Angela, his wonderful wife and business partner, who played a great role in the success of ALW.

CHAPTER 12

BOE ADAMS (MR. INSIDE)

I CAN'T TALK ABOUT ART WILLIAMS WITHOUT TALKING ABOUT his right-hand man, Boe Adams. Boe also proved to be one of the most influential mentors of my life. His work behind the scenes at ALW was invaluable, whether it was in raising investment capital, securing major carrier contracts, building headquarter office administrative infrastructure and personnel, or ultimately negotiating the sale of ALW. Boe and Art had met while Boe was with National Home Life Insurance Company. He had been charged by Art DeMoss, National Home's CEO, to build new distribution channels. When Boe and his wife, Myrna, relocated to Atlanta to begin their search for distribution partners, little did they know the great things that fate had in store for them.

While searching for new distribution partners, Boe met with Bob Turley, the former New York Yankee pitching great, who was one of Art's original seven Regional Vice Presidents (RVPs). Bob told Boe that instead of trying to recruit him, he needed him to talk to Art Williams, who was looking for a new insurance company to partner his whole team with. He also told Boe about some of the trials ALW was going through with state insurance regulators and the difficulties they faced finding an insurance carrier with the capacity for ALW's increasing business and future long-term goals.

Boe taught me how to be a businessman. He truly was one of the financial geniuses of our industry.

CHAPTER 13

HOW ONE DAY CHANGED
THE HISTORY OF FINANCIAL
SERVICES FOREVER

I LOOK BACK ON JANUARY 8, 1978, AS ONE OF THE MOST FATEFUL days in business history. It was a day that changed the arc of financial services history forever.

Four historic, industry-changing historic events happened on that day.

Historic Event No. 1: The State Insurance Department Gave ALW the Thumbs-Up

On that day, Art was in a hearing awaiting a decision from the Georgia Insurance Commissioner as to whether Art's new agency, ALW, would be allowed to remain in business. Art's philosophy of replacing the inadequate, small cash value policies being sold by the industry with his concept of Buy Term and Invest the Difference was totally disrupting how traditional life insurance was marketed. There was an unwritten rule in the industry (honor among thieves, you might call it) that agents should never replace another company's policies. Instead, they just sold them another normally inadequate policy. In reaction to Art's new approach, these traditional agents were putting tremendous pressure on the insurance commissioner. They were demanding that this replacement practice be stopped. Fortunately, on this day, Art received the thumbs-up from the commissioner that allowed ALW's legal and honorable crusade to continue and subsequently flourish.

Historic Event No. 2: ALW's Insurance Carrier Issued a Contract Termination Letter

At the time, ALW was writing business solely through the Financial Assurance Company (FAC). On that day, Art received a notice that FAC was terminating their contract with ALW because they didn't have the financial reserves to keep up with the sudden influx of business. Without an insurance carrier to underwrite their business and pay commissions, ALW would have literally had to close up shop. Thank goodness Boe Adams came along when he did, because he helped to provide the bridge between ALW and National Home Life Insurance. Fortunately for both parties, National Home was looking to move from the health insurance market into the life insurance market just as ALW had a growing need for their services.

Historic Event No. 3: Boe Adams and Art Williams Met for the First Time

With Bob Turley's encouragement, Boe met with Art that very day. Upon hearing about Art's positive Insurance Department ruling, and also about FAC's termination letter, Boe reached out to his boss at National Home, Art DeMoss, and convinced him to contract with ALW and provide them with the support they needed. This meant ALW was back in business.

Historic Event No. 4: Hubert Humphrey Joined ALW

The fourth historic event that happened on January 8, 1978, was my joining ALW. There I was, a little railroad conductor from Macon, who had been building his Amway business on the side, armed with a secret weapon and eager to join Art's crusade. Two powerful, disruptive forces were about to be unleashed on this old, stodgy, traditional industry. I brought a new viral recruiting and building system with me that would help deliver Art's industry-disrupting concept of Buy Term and Invest the Difference to the masses.

An all-powerful triumvirate had been formed with the alliance of these three players:

1. Art had the crusade.

2. Boe had all the financial expertise and connections.

3. Hubert had the distribution system.

Now you understand why I say that January 8, 1978, was unlike any other day. It literally changed the arc of financial services history (not to mention my career) forever.

CHAPTER 14

"THIS AIN'T NO AMWAY, BOY"

THE FIRST TIME I MET ART, THE FOUNDER OF A.L. WILLIAMS, was when he came to meet everyone at the Macon office. He showed up in his coaching shorts and a T-shirt. I had been in the business for only a week and had just come from a shift on the railroad. I was wearing my work clothes and work boots, but I made it a point to be there, regardless. Can you imagine how two future leaders in the financial services world—a football coach and a railroad conductor—looked at that first meeting? Coaching shorts and railroad clothes!

It turned out to be a great meeting, nevertheless. Art talked about how it was the best part-time opportunity out there and stated that he had one mission: to help people like me make money. This changed my life because no one had ever offered to really help me make money. As Art talked to us, I felt his passion. Right then and there, my simple, lifelong mission statement became evident: *To create wealth for those associates who joined us and for the clients who bought our concepts and products.*

When I think about this special moment, I'm reminded of a concept that has guided me many times over the years: *If the problem is big enough, and the solution is big enough, you can build one of the greatest success stories of all time.*

The *problem* was that the largest industry in the world, acting like the biggest bank in the world, was neglecting Middle America and selling mostly low-coverage, expensive cash value, whole life policies to Baby Boomers who mostly needed high-coverage, low-cost term insurance for that period of their lives. There was approximately $100 million in cash value whole life policies that needed to be replaced with term insurance. The *solution* was ultimately a combination of ALW's crusading concept of Buy Term and Invest the Difference and my Leadership Format System (LFS), which, as noted earlier, I had developed drawing from my Amway Multi-Level Marketing (MLM) era.

When I brought the Amway recruiting philosophy of "Sell the Dream and Build a Team" into the insurance industry, it really rocked the industry's boat. They quickly fought against us and labeled us as unprofessional.

Not only did we replace the insurance industry's business, we pulled the curtain back and showed the world what was really going on with them. They were the ones who were not professional. Our "non-professional" insurance agents were going to give the client three or four times the amount of coverage if the breadwinner died. Do you think a widow with four children would rather have a $200,000 death benefit from us or one or two expensive whole life policies worth $30,000 each, sold to her by a "professional" industry agent? Which one was professional? It was us. We embarrassed the industry and exposed them. The combination of the environment in America and the experience I brought from watching Amway grow gave me the confidence that ALW was going to succeed.

While Art shared his dream of ALW beating Prudential, the giant insurer, he didn't tell us exactly how we were going to make that happen. But his crusade became especially appealing to me when I realized the magnitude of the moment and that I had the vehicle needed to succeed.

He explained that his vision was to have three hundred thousand crusading agents across the country selling this concept. I was so fired up about it, I leaned over to ask the guy next to me how many agents we currently had. He answered, "About thirty." I quickly realized that passion without a system of distribution will only get you so far. Even though the guys at ALW didn't know it yet, they needed my distribution system. I saw a major opportunity.

During my first week in business leading up to that meeting, I was raring to start recruiting. I kept asking questions. I wanted to see the recruiting brochures and the motivational tools we were to use, and I pointed out all the different ways we recruited in the Amway business. I kept saying "Amway did this" and "Amway did that." Without realizing it, I was really rocking the boat.

By the time Art came by the office for that first meeting, word had already gotten back to him that I was running my mouth about Amway too much. At the end of that meeting, I saw my upline pointing me out to him. Art followed me out the door and introduced himself to me. He told me he appreciated my joining the company and then, as we were about to part, he pointed his finger at me and said in a firm though not mean way something I'll never forget: "Just remember, this ain't no Amway, boy."

It didn't register right away what he was saying, but a few days later I realized he wasn't a fan of Amway or multi-level marketing. I thought back on the week before and realized I had been spouting off about Amway quite a bit. From that time forward, I never mentioned the word "Amway" to Art again. But then I went on to build ALW into the "Amway of insurance and mutual funds."

In many ways, I was just like most people. I didn't want to *buy* insurance, much less *sell* insurance. I didn't even think I knew anybody to sell it to. But seventeen years of frustration on the railroad had built up such a desire in me to escape that dangerous life and create a new one where my dreams could come true, I knew I had to try. So, when I looked at this company in its infancy, all I could see was an opportunity to sell dreams and build teams like I had learned to do at Amway. Meanwhile, all the other ALW agents thought they were just in the insurance business.

History was being made. Unbelievably, this little Georgia Tech dropout and soon-to-be former railroad conductor became the first person to bring a network marketing (NWM) team-building, dream-selling system into the life insurance and financial services industry! We were saving two great business industries. By introducing this powerful new NWM distribution machine into the dying financial services sector, revitalizing it with new blood, we simultaneously legitimized the network marketing industry as a powerful new force for distribution.

CHAPTER 15

DISTRIBUTION IS KING— AND MY SYSTEM MADE ME KING OF DISTRIBUTION

THE STORY OF THE EARLY DAYS OF COCA-COLA REMINDS ME OF my early days with Art Williams. Just before his death in 1888, John Pemberton, the inventor of the tonic which later would be called Coca-Cola, sold his remaining interest in this unusual formula to Asa G. Candler for around $300. Candler was the only one who understood the drink and its fabulous potential. Shortly thereafter, he founded the great Coca-Cola company.

By focusing exclusively on soda fountain sales, he had become one of the country's great commercial success stories. But even Candler didn't have the vision for what would turn Coca-Cola into a worldwide giant in the bottling business.

It was actually two young, enterprising attorneys who had the ability to look to the future. Benjamin Thomas and Joseph Whitehead went to Candler with their idea to bottle Coca-Cola and sell it nationwide. This would make Coke portable and easily enjoyed by the masses. Bottling became the powerful distribution system that vaulted this beverage to its status as a global phenomenon.

The result surpassed their wildest dreams. Candler sold Thomas and Whitehead the rights to bottle Coca-Cola throughout nearly the entire US for the meager sum of one dollar. By the way, I actually saw a copy of this simple typewritten agreement at the World of Coca-Cola museum in Atlanta.

Candler simply did not envision the progress of the new century and never grasped the importance of the distribution system that would make Coca-Cola famous.

Art reminded me of Asa Candler. They both had a vision for their product, and they had the drive and passion, but without the right distribution system, their success could only go so far. I liken myself to Benjamin Thomas and Joseph Whitehead, who came along with a great distribution system that allowed unlimited success for a tremendously appealing preexisting product. I was inventing a whole new distribution system in the life insurance industry to deliver Art's great crusading message. Together, Art and I made an unstoppable and explosive team destined to change the biggest industry in the world.

He had a powerful warhead, but he needed my missile to deliver it to the target. Collectively, we were like a giant rocket ship with two great emotional-thrust engines—his powerful crusading concept and my powerful motivational team-building system.

Over the years, I would talk to Boe Adams about what I was trying to do, and he was pretty quick to see the vast potential of the System I would implement. He became a secret cheerleader for me and would often say with encouragement, "Hubert, don't just talk about it, go do it."

CHAPTER 16

READY...FIRE...AIM

MOST PEOPLE SPEND THEIR LIVES *GETTING STARTED, GETTING started.* Forever aiming and never pulling the trigger. That's not me. When I catch sight of an opportunity, I fire, ready or not. To quote General George Patton, "A good plan violently executed now is better than a perfect plan executed next week."[4]

Since it was clear that Art didn't really understand the Amway method of selling dreams and building teams, I patiently delayed launching the recruiting system I had learned there. For the first ninety days at ALW, I immersed myself in being a crusading personal producer and earned $28,000. This almost equaled my annual railroad salary, so I finally went full-time with ALW and quit the railroad. Once I was paid a 75 percent advance commission on the first-year annualized premium upon submission of the application, I caught the power and vision of magic multiples and money products.

I can't tell you how much this changed our lives. Finally, I had found the opportunity I'd been searching for. Norma just wanted to know two things: Was my new business legal? And was it going to last? She was tired of always being worried at the grocery store about what the total might be when she got to the checkout line. Frequently, she would fill up the shopping cart, see the bill rise as the cashier rang up each item, and then sheepishly have to ask to put some of the groceries back because we couldn't afford them all. Finally, the bill collectors stopped knocking on our door. In the years since then, we've been blessed to be able to live in beautiful homes, enjoy nice cars, travel the world, and, most of all, build financial security for our family and millions of others.

CHAPTER 17

THE POWER OF INEVITABILITY: DON'T WASTE WINDOWS OR MISS MARKETS

ONE OF MY FAVORITE WORDS IS *INEVITABLE,* WHICH MEANS *SURE and certain to happen*. I'm always looking for opportunistic waves of inevitability.

With this mindset, I attacked my dreams in each of the great companies we've built as if the outcomes were a forgone conclusion. Harnessing inevitability helps you become fearlessly relentless in your efforts to turn your dreams into reality. When *inevitable* joins with another word, the combination becomes even more powerful. Obviously *divine* inevitability is the most powerful because it reminds you of so much in your quest for eternal life, such as where you came from, why are you here, and where you are going.

The three two-word combinations I have used to my great business advantage are:

- Economic Inevitability
- Demographic Inevitability
- System Inevitability

Economic Inevitability

When ALW started in 1977, America was primed for a movement like ours. The country's dissatisfaction level was high because of the economics of that era. Inflation, unemployment, and government spending were all high. Conversely, economic growth, energy reserves, and the value of the dollar were low. Add to that such factors as gasoline shortages, the Iranian hostage crisis, and the proliferation of junk bonds, to name a few, and America in the late 1970s was left feeling as if our best days were behind us. To say there wasn't a lot of dreaming going on would be an understatement.

This served as a wake-up call for most Americans. Many were suffering and forced to look for an extra source of income. People who wouldn't have listened to us before were suddenly open to the opportunity. These conditions were ideal for our business. The circumstances created a perfect window of opportunity.

Fortunately, at this perfect moment, Art had just started the ALW Buy Term and Invest the Difference crusade to replace whole life insurance with cheaper term insurance and the investment of the savings in mutual funds. The insurance industry, which was the largest banking entity in the world, didn't want term insurance sold; they only wanted to sell cash value life insurance.

ALW is proof of the promise that *if the problem is big enough, and the solution is big enough, you can create one of the great businesses of all time.* You just have to be a part of that big solution, and that's where monster success comes from. The big problem with life insurance at that time was that one hundred million of the wrong kinds of policies were being sold, and nobody was selling any term insurance to Middle America. But when I realized this unique window of opportunity was open to us, our urgency to fill the void increased. We had mastered the right system, at the right time, in the right place. We were determined to ride this great economic wealth wave of inevitability like a surfer on the ocean. Over the next decade we went on to recruit 1.5 million people and sell over 10 million term policies, becoming the number one marketer of life insurance in the world.

When it finally dawned on me that this giant monolithic industry had become the largest in the world even though *nobody wanted to sell insurance and nobody wanted to buy it,* I knew that I was in the right place at the right time. This was one of the many waves of inevitability that I harnessed throughout my career.

Demographic Inevitability

Over the years, I have helped create many fortunes by recognizing industry-disrupting and wealth-transference windows, and aiming our powerful System at them. A line from Shakespeare's play *Julius Caesar* seems to sum up my thinking on this subject well: "There is a tide in the affairs of men. Which, taken at the flood, leads on to fortune; omitted, all the voyage of their life is bound in shallows and in miseries." [5] In fact, I've developed a mantra around this thinking: *Never waste windows and miss markets.*

What's vital to remember is that you don't create windows of opportunity; you can only recognize them and go through them. At ALW, as I've said earlier, we were luckily in the right place at the right time. Of course, I only learned this ten years later when I read Ken Dychtwald's book *Age Wave.* In it, he described the impact Baby Boomers—the generation of roughly 76 million people born between 1946 and 1964—would have during the next century. When World War II ended, sending all of the husbands back home, it created a baby boom, breaking a century-long US fertility decline. This age wave opened window after window, creating new market opportunities in every industry Boomers touched, first with baby foods and diapers, and later with retirement planning services and medical care. To paint a graphic picture of how Boomers would flood each subsequent marketplace en masse, Dychtwald likened them to a "pig going through a python."[6] That's exactly what was happening to the economy and society as the Boomers disrupted every industry they passed through. There was an enormous amount of money moving along with them, and we were positioned right in the middle of it.

At the time ALW was launched, people in this massive group were between the ages of twenty and thirty-four. They were at the early stages of adulthood and were entering the workforce, getting married, having children, and buying their first homes, cars, and, you guessed it, insurance.

As you can see, the Baby Boomers created demographic inevitability—they needed term life insurance, and nobody was selling it to them. That wasn't just a casual problem. That was our *big* problem. So, we attacked it with a vengeance. We built a business, enlisted an army of recruits, and followed the System I'd perfected. For me, it was the window of a lifetime, and I knew I was the right person, with the right vehicle, at the right time. The powerful combination of the Boomers' needs, our financial crusade, and my Leadership Format System totally changed the largest industry in the world—the insurance business—forever. All three of these powerful ingredients had to combine as we went through these windows, or we never would have built three great multibillion-dollar market cap companies. We were like Robin Hood, taking from the rich companies and giving back to Middle America.

System Inevitability

Our System was a *predictable, foolproof, profitable way for ordinary people to do extraordinary things*. This turnkey-format system provided a *duplicatable and transferable* way to easily allow a recruit to build a business that could break through the barriers that face traditional business owners.

A manned spacecraft needs three things to be successful:

1. The right conditions, or, as I call it, *an open window*
2. A well-prepared astronaut
3. A rocket ship (in other words, a distribution system) that reliably and predictably provides the thrust needed for the astronaut to break through the open window and resist the gravitational pull of the earth

System Inevitability comes from the predictability and speed with which you assimilate System knowledge throughout your whole organization. This is the secret of the Leadership Format System (LFS)—it is self-replicating, self-motivating, self-training, and self-financing.

CHAPTER 18

FROM POSSIBILITY THINKER TO IMPOSSIBILITY ACHIEVER

THE REASON I WAS SO PREPARED WHEN I WAS INTRODUCED TO the ALW opportunity was because I had learned a lot at Amway and was especially inspired by the story of Jim Janz. Jim had achieved Diamond Club status—a prestigious level in the organization—and was rewarded with a trip to Amway's private Diamond Club resort on Peter Island in the British Virgin Islands. He was feeling pretty good about his promotion until he discovered, upon his arrival, that he was just a small fish in a bigger pond. Many of the other guests on the island had achieved Amway's highest level at the time, Crown Diamond.

One evening Jim ran into Jay Van Andel (one of the founders of Amway) while walking on the beach. Their conversation changed Jim's life. Upon hearing Jim's frustrations that he was only a Diamond, Jay painted a picture of how Jim could earn his way up to the Crown Diamond level within the next six months. This would involve Jim understanding what his full potential was. Jay encouraged Jim to lay out a plan to make it happen. He also inspired Jim to become a *Possibility Thinker* by telling him about a book he had just finished reading, *Move Ahead with Possibility Thinking* by Robert H. Schuller. The book had given Jay a whole new way of thinking, and he knew it could do the same for others.

Jim was so inspired, he called his wife and told her about this exciting new *Possibility Plan*. He decided to leave the island immediately and spend most of the next six months visiting each of his leaders around Canada, stretching their vision just as his had been stretched. He showed them how it was possible for them to achieve their Crown Diamond status much faster than they had originally thought possible. Together, they could push the whole Janz team forward. Six months later, Jim Janz achieved Crown Diamond status! He had accomplished the seemingly impossible.

That story stuck with me. I took the idea of becoming a *Possibility Thinker* and expanded it into becoming an *Impossibility Achiever*. I realized that people who think things are seemingly impossible are often surpassed by people who are doing the very thing they thought to be impossible. From that point forward, I taught my teams about this great principle and helped them make the move from Possibility Thinkers to Impossibility Achievers.

Since that time, whenever I am asked how one becomes an Impossibility Achiever, I tell them to follow these ten sequential steps:

1. Raise your desire to 212 degrees.
2. Be willing to work.
3. Believe.
4. Commit 100 percent.
5. Rely on repetition and systems.
6. Develop know-how.
7. Trust in relentless inevitability.
8. Maintain a high FQ (failure quotient).
9. Have vision.
10. Be a Director of Motivation.

CHAPTER 19

IT ALL BEGAN WITH MY FIRST RECRUIT AT ALW: THE CHIP TAYLOR STORY

BEING A LEADER IN THE RECRUITING AND TEAM-BUILDING BUSI-ness is something I took very seriously, and it's something that comes with a lot of responsibility. To me, recruiting is the ulti-mate form of leadership. It's guiding a new team member from an old life into a new business. It's leading them from one para-digm to another and giving them a system that affords them the best chance at success. From my very first recruit, Chip Taylor, I felt the weight of that leadership responsibility.

He was a dreamer just like me. On one of our trips around Middle Georgia, Chip and I stopped at a Pizza Hut when it opened and ended up staying there all day, brainstorming about ways to be more efficient with our time. We had started to make pretty good commissions. I sold him on the bigger idea that we could each make $50,000 in the next ninety days by figuring out how to *collapse time frames* and *compress activity*. We did two things that day. First, we spent three hours brainstorming and devel-oping our prospect list. Then, we developed the *Speed Calendar*, which I've used for over forty years in building all three of our revolutionary companies.

I learned from a verse in Psalms that "a thousand years on earth is but a day in the sight of the Lord" (a paraphrase of Psalm 90:4). What a powerful paradigm. While we'll never be able to collapse time like our Heavenly Father, we can become

Possibility Thinkers and Impossibility Achievers by compressing a decade into one year, one year into three months, three months into one week, one week into one day, and one day into three mini-days.

Inspired by this concept, we determined how we could get eighteen mini-days out of every week and be able to rest on Sunday. It was simple; we could *invent* more time by dividing every day into three mini-days:

Mini-Day One - From 7:00 a.m. until noon

Mini-Day Two - From noon until 6:00 p.m.

Mini-Day Three - From 6:00 p.m. until midnight

I once had a conversation with one of my competitors who had read my Leadership Format System (LFS) book and was intrigued by this powerful new calendar idea. He looked at me and said, "Well, no wonder we can't beat your team. You've got a different calendar."

Chip quickly brought in and developed some excited new recruits. Among them were Gary Lee and Bill McCord. They were energetic and willing to do whatever it took to succeed. They would prove to be an effective part of my national expansion in the near future.

CHAPTER 20

DO WHAT SUCCESS REQUIRES

AFTER EIGHTEEN MONTHS AT ALW, I HAD QUALIFIED TO BECOME a *Regional Vice President (RVP)*, helping the company to expand nationally. This meant moving from Macon, the place where my entire family was born and raised. We'd have to leave friends and parents, familiar and loved places, and the culture we had grown up in throughout our entire lives. There is a special place reserved in heaven for my sweet wife, Norma, for enduring all the things I put her and the family through on this journey. I moved her away from her parents while we had four kids. My eldest, Jody, would change schools his senior year, just as he was on the verge of making the varsity basketball team. Kim was twelve and leaving the only home she'd ever known. Jeffrey was nine, and our youngest, Jennifer, was six. Norma had no idea what the house or neighborhood we were moving to even looked like because I had picked it out a month earlier on my first trip to Denver. But all the family supported me because they realized this was a great opportunity and I was prepared to do whatever it took to win.

The only two states Art was sending new RVPs to were Texas and Louisiana, because those were the only states that offered a temporary license for new recruits besides Georgia. His whole game plan was getting new greenies off to a fast start in sales. But since my main focus was selling the dream instead of just selling insurance, I knew I could succeed in any state quickly, because it takes no license to sell dreams. Despite Art adamantly pushing for me to go to one of these fast-start, temporary-licensing states, I told my upline RVP that I was going to move to Denver, Colorado. Thinking that he had cleared this choice with Art at the company headquarters, I went forward with my plan. I chose to move to Denver because it was a booming population center, and it felt like the Atlanta of the West. In fact, it was the major airline hub for the West.

CHAPTER 21

IGNORANT ENTHUSIASM:
THE GLENN MILLS STORY

ABOUT NINETY DAYS BEFORE I WAS SCHEDULED TO MOVE FROM Macon to Denver, I recruited Glenn Mills, a new member of our church congregation whose company had just transferred him from Raleigh to Macon.

Right away he asked me a lot of questions and shadowed me to meetings and appointments to learn more about this business opportunity. He was intrigued. He asked me if I would let him join. He was full of excitement when he signed up, but, unfortunately, since he was so new in the area, he didn't get much traction. He kept assuring me that he had a lot of friends and contacts who would listen to him back in North Carolina. I told him that we would look into that sometime in the future.

Because he was determined to show me he could succeed, Glenn went back to Raleigh, his hometown, without telling me, so he could meet with people he knew. A few days later he informed me that he had thirty prospects excited to join our company. Even though I was moving to Denver the next week, I agreed to hold an opportunity meeting for him in Raleigh right away. Because he had that most powerful ingredient of all—Ignorant Enthusiasm—we were able to recruit all thirty people and close over thirty sales to launch his career.

Glenn is a great example of how a Driven, Determined Dreamer took our System, in its raw form, and sold the dream to so many others. His success illustrates the power of Ignorant

Enthusiasm as well as the power of *Stumbling Forward* and *Staying Confused*. Glenn achieved the success he longed for, becoming my very first RVP and first $100,000-ring earner. His story didn't stop there, as you will discover in a later chapter. From this unlikely start came one of my greatest leaders ever.

Remember, *it only takes a small spark to ignite a great future.*

CHAPTER 22

FAILURE IS NOT AN OPTION

ONCE AGAIN, I CHOSE "THE ROAD LESS TRAVELED BY." IN THE summer of 1979, I loaded the moving truck with everything we had and hitched a trailer to the back for my newly purchased used Cadillac. Norma and the kids piled in our old station wagon with a small U-Haul attached to carry whatever didn't fit in the moving truck.

We hadn't even made it a mile when our future was almost derailed. We stopped by Norma's parents to say goodbye one last time—something I really didn't want to do because I knew how upset her mom was with me for taking her little girl and her grandbabies to Denver. But we stopped anyway and, while I was there, I made one last call to the local office before hitting the road. They told me that there was an urgent message from Art. He wanted to meet me in Atlanta within the next two hours!

I replied we were all packed up and ready to hit the road. None of that mattered. I had to meet him where he was. This meant taking my car off the trailer, leaving my family at Norma's parents' house, and driving to a Denny's restaurant somewhere in northern Atlanta. I had no idea why I had been summoned so urgently.

I arrived to find Art and Boe waiting on me. The fact that Boe was there meant the topic must be serious. As I mentioned earlier, Boe was Art's right-hand man. We called him "Mr. Inside." In the years to come, he would become a dear friend and mentor to me. I distinctly remember seeing Art and Boe sitting there eating patty melts. Art congratulated me on qualifying for RVP and told me that he had heard we were thinking about moving to Denver. It was apparent then that he'd just assumed I was moving to Texas. I told him that we were beyond the thinking stage. We were packed up and had actually departed when I'd gotten the call to come meet them.

This seemed to surprise Art. Remember, his initial game plan was to recruit greenies and get them off to a fast start in one of the three states—Georgia, Texas, or Louisiana—that allowed temporary licenses at the time. He told me that the company really needed me to go to Texas. Bob White had been sent to San Antonio, Jack Schuman to Houston, Bill Orender to Dallas, and Ron Wright to New Orleans. If I moved to Texas, I would be just another RVP operating the same way as everyone else—as an eagle in a chicken coop. I needed to be where my System could take hold and grow.

I couldn't really tell Art I was going out there to build an empire by selling dreams because that sounded too much like Amway. With Boe's help, I was able to persuade Art that this was a good idea. Boe understood I was selling dreams while everyone else was selling insurance. Since he knew that my recruiting and building System was what the company needed, he pushed hard for me to have the opportunity to make it work in Denver and throughout the West.

After I had Art's approval, he taught me a life lesson for which I'm forever indebted to him. He told me that right now I had two options: fail or succeed, but once I accepted the RVP position and moved to Denver, I was forfeiting failure as an option. From that point forward in my career, I only had one option—TO SUCCEED. Art made it clear that the company could not afford to have an RVP fail. Failure was unacceptable.

Art had an idea whose time had come—to mount the Buy Term and Invest the Difference crusade. But I had another idea whose time had come—to launch a revolutionary generational team-building system in the life insurance industry. I had kept this secret under wraps while in Macon so I wouldn't get pushback from Art. Sitting on the secret was like having a winning poker hand. I had to keep my poker face so I wouldn't tip my hand. As I predicted, we exploded in Denver. I built a giant, record-setting Base Shop that became the duplication model for the rest of the company. I shared my secrets in my first book, *The Magic of Compound Recruiting*, which has sold over a million copies and been used industrywide.

This was a pivotal moment in my life. I'm forever thankful that I chose "the road less traveled by." I was the keeper of a secret that had now officially launched the Amway of the insurance industry.

It became clear to me that many people would claim they were willing to do whatever it took, but very few were actually willing to pay the price. I was tremendously motivated by the knowledge that in moving to Denver, I would be pioneering the company's westward expansion, turning it into a national powerhouse.

The dawning of a new distribution model in an old industry.

Since we were at ground level, the team-building compensation structure hadn't been developed yet, so I had to rely on what I'd learned at Amway to create a modified version to fit the moment. Originally, RVP was the highest level in the company, but I was able to help influence the company to build a powerful networking-type compensation and promotion ladder. This allowed the greenies we had just recruited to quickly start recruiting a team of their own. Shortly after receiving their licenses and sales training, they were overriding[7] their team's production. We began creating new levels, such as Senior Vice President (SVP), National Sales Director (NSD), and Senior National Sales Director (SNSD), and we instituted all-company bonus pools, great incentive trips, and many other powerful initiatives.

In short, we shifted the paradigm. We were no longer just an aggressive insurance agency using part-timers; we were a team-building, dream-selling powerhouse that, as I mentioned earlier, recruited more than 1.5 million people and sold over 10 million term life policies. We completely disrupted the whole industry with our revolutionary distribution model. We were the first to combine *multiples* and *money products*. The industry didn't know what had hit them. Before we upended the market, the average age of a traditional insurance agent was approximately fifty-eight. And more agents were leaving the industry than new ones were joining. Our approach literally saved this declining industry by pumping a constant flow of new agent recruits into it.

CHAPTER 23

LET YOUR FRUSTRATION FUEL YOU

WHEN I WAS BORN, THE DOCTOR HELD ME UP BY MY FEET AND slapped my rear end, but he didn't stamp *railroad man* on my butt. That was not going to be my destiny. I could be anything I wanted to be. Yes, the railroad provided a solid job with benefits. Yes, it was the kind of job considered enviable in a blue-collar town like Macon. And no, people didn't just up and leave a job like that. But I eventually awakened from this accidental career I had become trapped in after dropping out of college. Looking back, I realized I had learned a lot of life lessons during those seventeen years in that job, and I'd built up a tremendous amount of frustration dream fuel too.

When I told everyone that I was quitting and we were leaving Macon, they all thought I was crazy, especially my railroad buddies. Nobody took me seriously. To be fair, I had run my mouth several times before about how I was getting into another new business. I was sure that each one was going to be my escape ticket from the railroad, only to be disappointed. Even though I had friends, coworkers, and family telling me I was crazy and that I should just stop trying to get out, my mind was made up. I'd learned the truth of the adage, "Nothing is more powerful than a made-up mind," by Lewis Gordon.[8] I had made up my mind, and nothing was going to stop me from trying.

A strange thing happened soon afterward that reminded me of how grateful I was that I never stopped dreaming of a better life for me and my family. Even though I had officially quit the railroad two years earlier, I received a call from a new rookie crew dispatcher wanting me to "mark back up" from the "off board" and return to work since they were short of personnel. I had to explain that I had quit and was now living in Denver. This caused me to realize how far I'd come in only a couple of years. Because I kept my Trying Motor going, I was able to move full steam ahead on this great new opportunity. Gone were the days of getting calls like that from a scheduler putting me on another long, dangerous job. They had controlled my time, but they never controlled my mind or heart. I could have easily stayed at my secure job and let life pass me by, but I didn't. I was so thankful that I'd had the courage to take that giant leap of faith and go *ALL IN*. I had declared my intentions to be great, regardless of what anyone thought, and had backed up my decision with action.

I'm sure there were people still in Macon wondering what had happened to old Hubert, probably saying things like, "Is he off chasing some silly dream again?" "I'm sure he'll be back," or "No one from around these parts makes it big." But I had prepared myself so when the right window opened, I would be able to recognize it and blast right through it. To paraphrase an old saying, *Reach for the stars, else what is a heaven for?* Don't ever let anybody else steal your dreams.

Years later, legendary NBA head coach Pat Riley described the path to success this way:

> *"From Nobody to Upstart ...*
> *From Upstart to Contender ...*
> *From Contender to Winner ...*
> *From Winner to Champion ...*
> *From Champion to Dynasty."* [9]

That is exactly how I see my ladder of success evolution. I had started as an unknown, but before long I became a dynasty by helping other key leaders build their dynasties.

CHAPTER 24

OVERCOMING OBSTACLES ON THE ROAD TO SUCCESS

I HEADED OUT TO DENVER EXCITED ABOUT OUR FUTURE. I WAS super confident that this wonderful new ALW opportunity would provide me with the perfect platform to unleash my Leadership Format System (LFS). Just as I was leaving, the company was about to sign a big ten-year deal with National Home Life (NHL) to build a dedicated home office in Atlanta just for ALW. By the time I got to Denver three days later and called Boe Adams as planned, he shared that Art DeMoss, the founder and CEO of NHL, had died unexpectedly on a tennis court two days earlier. He explained that the DeMoss family estate had decided not to move forward on the deal with ALW since they were going to sell NHL, but Boe calmed me down by telling me that he had been working his magic in the background. This secret plan B would turn out to be an even better option. He quickly signed a new deal with a company called Penn Corp and simultaneously negotiated a six-month workout extension on the NHL closeout. Penn Corp set up a dedicated office for us in Atlanta, and we were able to make the adjustment to this new insurance carrier on the fly. Even while all of that was going on, I continued selling dreams, front-end loading my business, and building teams.

I learned that all of the challenges we go through in life are for our own good and to give us experience.

The main lesson is that I had made a total commitment; I had burned all the boats, so to speak. I was constantly inspired by Art's challenge as I was leaving to open up Denver and the territory of the West: *Failure is totally unacceptable.* I had to succeed at all costs.

Don't let anything hold you back. It's your choice to succeed or fail. You can win in spite of any obstacle you face. I was part of something bigger than myself, which gave me the strength and the courage to focus on the main things. Experience is the key to greatness.

CHAPTER 25

NATIONAL EXPANSION

During the first six months in Denver, my team was growing rapidly. I knew I needed more leadership help. It was the right time to finally have Chip Taylor, Bill McCord, and Gary Lee come out to Denver to be my wingmen. They excitedly hit the road and headed West.

After a couple of weeks of not hearing from them, I wondered what had happened. It turns out they took the southern route to Colorado, which led through the city of Pueblo, where they stopped to pick up some equipment from Radio Shack for our meetings. While they were there, they ended up recruiting the store manager, John Cantwell. Before they knew it, they had recruited seven or eight more people that week to work with John, planting the ALW flag in that city. Chip, Bill, and Gary were a tight-knit three-man team that acted as one.

Chip finally called and told me the whole story. Things were going so well they had decided to stay there and open up the Pueblo area! Their focus on recruiting new greenies was a great example of the power of *Ignorant Enthusiasm.* They stumbled forward and stayed confused, just putting one foot in front of the other.

Together we developed John Cantwell and his team into a strong RVP center. Now it was time for me to move them to Denver. This freed me up to start opening and training people in dozens of satellite offices around the West while Chip and Bill and Gary filled in for me in our big recruiting and training meetings.

Even though they were very excited and motivated, it was clear to me that, as a group, they were doing the work one great leader could do alone. It was time to divide and conquer. I taught them the System they would ultimately use to become great Super Team builders. I was expanding and sending leaders all over the country. I sent Chip to Kansas City, Bill to St. Louis, and Gary to Idaho. This allowed me to open up three great new areas.

I've learned many times that a plant can only grow to its full potential if it's repotted in more fertile soil. I applied this repotting principle to myself when I moved from Macon to Denver. I blossomed there in ways I never could have in Macon. I knew firsthand that this principle worked, so I uprooted many of our strongest leaders and sent them across the nation to open up the Humphrey National Network (HNN) for ALW.

It took about sixteen months to build the Denver foundation, and then another six months for it to really take off. By the end of twenty-three months in Denver, we had recruited twenty-four thousand people and satellited leaders into about twenty-five states. To put this in perspective, when we moved to Denver, there were around seven to eight hundred people in the entire company. It didn't take long for other key ALW leaders to visit us in Denver and learn the secrets of our explosive growth. They started to copy my System prototype, taking it back to their areas of the country for implementation. This caused massive exponential growth at ALW of over two hundred thousand new agents during the course of the next two years.

CHAPTER 26

ENTICE AND WITHDRAW: THE JACK AND LINDA LINDER STORY

WHEN I FIRST HEADED TO DENVER TO LAUNCH THE GREAT ALW expansion, I felt I had the chance of a lifetime to finally be somebody and to show the world what I could do.

I left to build my business knowing only one person who lived in Denver. I had ninety more referrals from family, friends, and business associates back in Macon, but I only knew one person where I was headed. Upon learning that I was moving, my sister Sandra called me the night before we hit the road to refer two friends of hers—Jack and Linda Linder from Austin. Jack had just been transferred by his company to Denver but was desperately looking for a way to get back to his roots in Texas. He became number ninety-one on my list.

The main reason I had the confidence to make this signif- icant move to Denver was because I had solved the industry's biggest problem: prospecting. I had developed my *Friendship Farming* strategy, which turned strangers into friends; my *Friendship Borrowing* strategy, which allowed me to share in the friendship relationships of others; and my Leadership Format System (LFS) strategy, which allowed me to geometrically build teams of dream sellers.

Every person who has ever been born on this earth desires more, which makes them a prospect. The word *enthusiasm* comes from the Greek word *entheos*, which means *God within*.[10] Every human being who has ever been created—or will ever be created in the future—by our Heavenly Father is born with this great power. All we have to do is activate this power that's embedded within all of us. The sad thing is, most people go through life never having activated it. In my efforts to get people to do this for themselves, I have learned that it is human nature for people to jump to conclusions—and usually the wrong conclusions. So, when presenting people with the opportunity, *my main objective is to control the conclusion to which they are likely to jump.* One of the most effective ways I've learned to accomplish this involves a secret control strategy. I have found that by simultaneously activating their *Greed Button* by mentioning money possibilities (note: there is both *good* and *bad* greed in this world), and their *Curiosity Button* by holding back the full explanation until the right time, I can lead them to the right conclusion.

One of the best examples I've ever had of this working was when I went to visit Jack Linder, number ninety-one on my referral list. Late one evening at around ten o'clock, I was returning from an appointment, and I realized I was near where Jack lived, so I swung by and introduced myself. When he answered the door of his apartment, it was obvious that he and his wife were preparing to go to bed and weren't expecting visitors.

It was a little awkward at first because a stranger had just knocked on their door late in the evening, but when I told them that Sandra Ottley was my sister, they let their guard down and invited me in. Jack was naturally curious about why I was there. I explained that Sandra suggested I stop by and tell him about the business I was starting in Denver. I began by hitting his Greed Button. We talked about my prior few years and how I'd gone from working on the railroad and making very little money to finding ALW and earning $105,000 working part-time in my first twelve months. This got Jack's attention because it was roughly what he was making after twenty years at his job. I went on, sharing that after eighteen months with ALW, I was now making about $400,000 a year.

Next, I hit his Curiosity Button by dropping hints about Texas. I told him I was in Denver for one reason: to open up the West and find great leaders. I stayed focused on the success that my other new expansion leaders and I were having. I didn't give him too many details about the company, but I very subtly mentioned that I was looking to open up Texas in the near future, all the while knowing that he desperately wanted to get back there to take care of some of his business enterprises, including a cattle ranch.

As I continued the conversation about this crusade, Jack kept coming back to the topic of Texas. He asked who was opening the state. I told him we hadn't identified the right leader yet, and then I changed the subject. By using the old fisherman's technique of Entice and Withdraw, I lured him to bite the hook and recruit himself. Next, I invited him to an Opportunity Meeting scheduled for the following night. Unlike most executives who were content with their twenty-year corporate career, Jack was not satisfied, nor was he afraid to take risks. He came to the meeting, liked what he saw, and the rest is history.

Jack wanted in and before he'd even been trained, been on an appointment, or had a license, he quit his $100,000-a-year job and made plans to move back to Texas! I was surprised he was ready to go that fast. I laid out a success plan for him with a thirty-day goal of holding a meeting in Austin with his first thirty prospects. I told him to do just what I had done to him—activate their Curiosity and Greed Buttons. I told him to aim for thirty ambitious people who were looking for an opportunity.

Before Jack and Linda left Denver for Austin, I asked Norma, my spouse and business secretary at the time, to gather some start-up supplies for him to take to Texas to help open his business. After a while she came back with a box full of NHL life insurance applications and about a hundred pee bottles! Back then, when we would write up a client application, we had to collect a urine specimen in a little bottle and send it along with the application to the insurance company. I don't think Jack had envisioned collecting specimen bottles as part of this new opportunity. The main thing I got him focused on was the power of our System. I gave him a copy of my LFS, which I had written out by hand for him, including the Six Steps and Eight Speed Filters, and I told him that I'd see him in thirty days at our Austin kickoff.

Jack's first meeting with his top thirty prospects was a huge success. We recruited them all and closed many sales. After his fast start, I returned and helped him open our first Texas office in Austin.

One of the most powerful lessons I learned from my days at Amway was how to become a student of human nature. During my first few years, I had almost no success getting people to listen to me, and I couldn't understand why. Then it came to my mind that a great hunter or a great fisherman certainly has to understand the nature of the beast. I remembered in the Scriptures how Jesus *recruited* Peter and his brothers to become the first disciples. They were fishermen by trade. Jesus told them to put down their nets. He said, "Follow me, and I will make you fishers of men" (Matthew 4:19 KJV). It now became clear to me that I needed something to help save me from myself while I was mastering the art of approaching new prospects. So, I developed the guide below, Hubert's Ten Keys to Human Nature:

1. Humans are quick to jump to conclusions.
2. They're skeptical.
3. They procrastinate. (Their spirit is willing, but their flesh is weak.)
4. They're greedy. (They dream of great wealth.)
5. They're curious.
6. They don't think they can sell.
7. They don't like salespeople.
8. They would like to be their own boss.
9. They would like to have a business of their own, *BUT...*
10. They all doubt they ever could or would have that business.

Jack and his wife, Linda, became some of our greatest friends. Jack was an elite member of my *Inner Circle*. He chose to build his exceptional team mainly in Texas, with a few offices around the country. He was very focused on making sure his teammates made money and were successful. I could have easily overlooked Jack at first, thinking that he was making enough of an income and assuming he wouldn't be interested in another business, but I let him make that decision. I discovered a long time ago that I'm not a mind reader and I can't tell what's in people's hearts. So, I learned how to press the right buttons at the right time, helping to launch the careers of Jack and many other great leaders.

Remember, *it only takes a small spark to ignite a great future.*

CHAPTER 27

A SYSTEM CAN SAVE YOU
FROM YOURSELF

IN MICHAEL E. GERBER'S BESTSELLING BOOK *THE E-MYTH: WHY Most Small Businesses Don't Work and What to Do About It*, there is a great line that perfectly sums up the importance of systems:

> For ordinary people to do extraordinary things, a system—"a way of doing things"—is absolutely essential in order to compensate for the disparity between the skills your people have and the skills your business needs if it is to produce consistent results.[11]

I had learned from my Amway days that the biggest stars keep things simple. So, I had an adage: *Simplify to Multiply*. By staying focused on my System, I would have enough time for my efforts to compound into great teams.

The letter I accidentally received from Bill Campbell with those few intriguing words written on it became the guiding principle of the System I ran throughout my career. I loved it precisely because it was simple. When we recruited someone, that's what they were told to run. I eventually added eight filters to further improve results, but the System hasn't changed in decades. I've always loved the idea of aligning with something that was much bigger than myself. A simple system can be just that.

The magic of a system is that *it saves you from yourself*. This is such an important point that it bears repeating: *A system saves you from yourself*. It rescues you from distractions, boredom, and the temptation to wander off into the world of unimportant things. It gets you to just stick to the basics.

A system is the great equalizer. Suddenly you don't have to be everything to everyone; you just have to run the system. It allows you to be in business for yourself, but not by yourself. You run the system. The system runs the business. The system is what allows you to have a great quality of life.

In February of 1981, I held a big meeting at the Sheridan Tech Center in Denver, where we ended up getting caught in a massive storm. We were snowed in and couldn't leave the hotel. The meeting was all about the importance of mastering our Leadership Format System. Prior to the meeting, I had ordered about one hundred copies of the book *Grinding It Out: The Making of McDonald's* by Ray Kroc. Since I had a captive audience, I spent the next two days drilling into their minds the importance of the McDonald's Franchise Format System. Kroc made sure his franchises were formatted to work *every time*. It had to be predictable, foolproof, profitable, and even idiotproof. My team needed to learn the value of running our System as exactly as McDonald's ran theirs.

I firmly believe the best kind of leaders are *System Leaders*. Anyone, from any walk of life, can quickly be turned into a leader if there is a success system they can align with. Businesses run by System Leaders have much more upside and are more predictable, profitable, and duplicatable than businesses run by personality-driven leaders without a system.

I've always taught new recruits that to succeed at the highest level, they must have these two things: *a passion for our mission* and *a submission to our System*. The ability to achieve success is in everyone, but very few can self-activate the greatness lying dormant inside.

It's easier to activate and achieve when we align ourselves with something bigger than ourselves and submit to a proven system. The principle that *DISCIPLINE and ACCOUNTABILITY lead to ASCENSION and DOMINANCE* is hardwired into the System.

Teaching accountability is a mechanism that keeps score. I always drove myself to become the dominant player on our company's leaderboard, and in doing so, my example challenged many of our stars to fight every month for ascension up the leaderboard too.

This provided the perfect combination of *something to aim for* and *the competitive drive to win*. I taught our people two things: *If you aim at nothing, you'll hit it!* and *Shoot for the stars, else what is a heaven for?*

Ever since I perfected the System in Denver, I have never stopped using and championing its success principles. The US Marine Corps adopted the saying "Kill 'em all and let God sort 'em out," so I borrowed that saying and applied it to our business: "Recruit 'em all and let the System sort 'em out." Art Williams taught me that there has never been a device or machine invented that can look into the heart of a man or woman to see if they are a winner. I was a product of the System. The System sorted me out and gave me a chance to put my drive and determination to work. The same would prove true for all of our great leaders who emerged to build the great teams of our companies.

I have never stopped using and championing the System's success principles. I'm a walking, talking example of how following a system can lead to massive team-building success. *The rapid, relentless repetition of the System's six simple recruiting and building steps can lead to a giant, successful distribution team.* This *Six-Step Leadership Format System* (sometimes referred to as the *Six Steps*) will lead to the *continuous opening of outlets,* while the *Eight Speed Filters* I added will result in the *simultaneous flow of production through the outlets*. The magic of the process is driven by these three *System Engines*:

- System Engine One: *Recruiter's Mentality*
- System Engine Two: *Builder's Mindset*
- System Engine Three: *Director of Motivation*

The engines are designed to produce maximum efficiency and results when they are run sequentially, in unison, and perpetually. They are the success keys of the Leadership Format System.

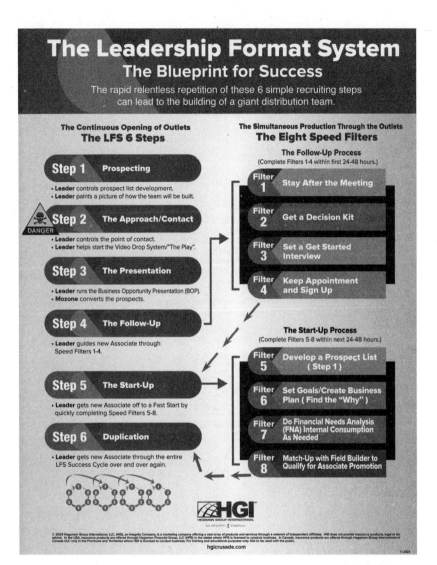

CHAPTER 28

SYSTEM ENGINE ONE:
A RECRUITER'S MENTALITY

The System begins with a Recruiter's Mentality. It doesn't start with a sales mentality. Recruiting is an all-the-time thing. It is a state of mind. The idea is to look for a quantity of prospects, and somewhere in that mix you will find quality prospects. The System was conceived to help you compound from the *Law of Averages* to the *Law of High Numbers*. The System always leads the prospect through its Six Steps and Eight Speed Filters. The prospect will either come out of the steps as a recruit and a client or simply as a satisfied client. We offer each prospect an education on the following six financial principles:

1. Increased Cash Flow
2. Debt Management
3. Emergency Funds
4. Proper Protection
5. Building Wealth
6. Preserving Wealth

Every prospect is a recruit until proven differently. Recruiting means leading with the *opportunity* and the *dream*. Next comes a *Financial Needs Analysis (FNA)* for each new prospect, followed by a *Solutions-Based Sale* to those we recruited and also to the prospects we didn't recruit, based on what they need and can afford. We abide by the ancient philosophy of Lao Tzu, the founder of Taoism. A proverb often attributed to Lao Tzu says, "If you give a hungry man a fish, you feed him for a day, but if you teach him how to fish, you feed him for a lifetime." To explain this in my own terms, *Sell a person a policy and they'll benefit for a while. Teach them a concept with a sale and they'll benefit for a lifetime.*

By sharing our business opportunity with them at the outset, we address the first and most important principle in their financial education: *Increased Cash Flow*. This principle is so simple, but so many people get it wrong: *Aim at Recruits and Hit Sales.*

System Assimilation—the speed and exactness with which you copy the System—will determine your success. This precise cookie-cutter approach must be duplicated throughout your team. In many ways, recruits are the raw material we put through our System with the goal of having them come out on the other side as a *finished product* or a trained leader building his or her own business. We fondly refer to this process as our *RMD (Regional Marketing Director) Factory.*

While learning and mastering how to build my financial services team, I discovered two truths: *Width = Profitability* and *Depth = Security and Stability*. In other words, when you are casting for a constant stream of new recruits, going *wide fast* assures that you have significant cash flow as you develop your downlines. This *perpetual speed width* provided me with a much greater diversification of risk, almost like a human mutual fund. It's a more secure and stable approach than any other I know. The *security and stability* are developed by continuously *Taprooting* through each new recruit and always applying *Overlapping Leadership* to develop leaders at all levels. Taprooting is designed to assist leaders in making sure that each new recruit, no matter their level, is consistently bringing in new recruits. I built and sustained a leadership factory with a great Base Shop (my personal team), where I trained people to become great system leaders (RMDs) who did the same. I like to say I was *perpetually pregnant* with new RMD trainee candidates.

Simply put, having a Recruiter's Mentality means:

- Personal recruiting NEVER STOPS!
- Base Shop recruiting NEVER STOPS!
- Super Team recruiting NEVER STOPS!

Recruiting is basically the procurement of raw materials to the building site, just as a building contractor secures supplies from a building supply center. Until you lead the new recruit through the System, they are still just raw material.

CHAPTER 29

SYSTEM ENGINE TWO: A BUILDER'S MINDSET

MY LEADERS AND I WERE IN THE BUSINESS OF BUILDING THOU-sands of System Leaders. We had a *Builder's Mindset*. We saw ourselves constructing a large network of system leaders who were duplicating our success with a large base of diversified, product-using clients of their own. *Every day was dedicated to completing this vision.* This is a different mindset than just being a recruiter. This requires having a *massive change of attitude*, a *mighty burst of energy*, and a *willingness to make an aggressive vertical move*.

As we were continuously *Going Wide*, we were also *Going Deep*, naturally Taprooting—connecting with, mentoring, and coaching our downline associates. Through this Overlapping Leadership style, we produced System Leaders who replicated downline System Leaders at each level, thereby applying the principle of *Depth = Security and Stability*. As we worked with leaders and their teams, the System naturally brought the cream to the top. It filtered out the weak and rewarded the strong. Some of my greatest leaders came from going deep. It didn't matter how far down the line the rising leaders were, I would work with them and develop them. I was *generation blind*—I didn't focus on the percent of commission I would be making from their efforts.

The System allowed us to build a business whereby recruiting, building, and production never stopped. It was self-replicating. Like anything great that has been built, it was built three times.

It was built in someone's mind first, then it was put down on paper in great detail, and finally, it was actually built to last. It was no different than building a great team.

The following three *Laws of Duplication* separate the great Builders from the Recruiters:

1. A *Recruit* isn't a Recruit until he or she has a Recruit.
2. A Recruit does not become a *Leg* until it is four Recruits deep.
1. A Leg will become a *Team*, with a life of its own, once at least two Leaders are developed.

I have always said that great things can happen when you go four deep. Consider the powerful four-deep example of Socrates to Plato to Aristotle to Alexander the Great. They conquered and changed the whole world!

Just because a building contractor has all of the raw material delivered to his or her building site, he or she can't expect the material to magically assemble itself into a building. That takes getting the blueprints, securing financing, assembling the construction crew, and beginning the building process. The same is true in our business. You can't just recruit someone and expect them to become a leader all by themselves. You have to guide them through the System's Six Steps and Eight Speed Filters. And repeat this same cycle over and over with each wave of new downline recruits.

A Builder's Mindset is the higher law:

Higher Law	vs.	Lesser Law
Aims at building leadership teams	vs.	Aims at achieving titles
It's how you feel	vs.	Not what you know

Higher Law	vs.	Lesser Law
Builds and directs dynasties	vs.	Runs a dynasty
Will	vs.	Skill
Leader of People	vs.	Manager of Things
Be a Kingmaker	vs.	Be a King
TEAM over ME Mentality	vs.	ME Mentality

Simply put, having a Builder's Mindset means:
- Personal Width Building of Direct Leaders NEVER STOPS!
- Base Shop Taprooting Construction through Direct Leaders NEVER STOPS!
- Super Team Overlapping Leadership Development NEVER STOPS!

CHAPTER 30

SYSTEM ENGINE THREE:
DIRECTOR OF MOTIVATION

BEING A *DIRECTOR OF MOTIVATION* IS ESSENTIALLY THE ENERGY source fueling the first two Leadership Format System engines. No one is born to be a great motivator, but the System can instill that ability in them. I always pointed my team to the great motivators and put them in the right settings and meetings to be influenced and have their vision stretched. That's how I became a Director of Motivation myself. I knew that my team would only rise to the level of their vision. So, sending them to exciting events and putting them in front of leaders who could stretch their vision in ways I couldn't do alone was a top priority. I loved using the *Magic of Crowds*. People will only change after having a significant emotional experience, and that occurs in meetings like ours all the time.

As I said earlier, I could always recognize the great leaders by seeing who and how many others followed them to events. RECRUIT...BUILD...MOTIVATE!

To become legends in our business, my leaders had to master the art of communication with large groups of people at all levels. They worked with every leader as if they were first generation to them.

Simply put, being a Director of Motivation means:
- Constant Personal Communication with your *Direct Leaders* NEVER STOPS!

- Constant Personal Communication with your Base Shop Leaders NEVER STOPS!
- Constant Personal Communication with your Super Team Leaders NEVER STOPS!

Being a Director of Motivation also means mastering the art of communication, whether you are interacting with one individual or with large groups of people at all levels.

You must be able to:

- Hold big recognition events
- Send letters, emails, texts, and other personal forms of correspondence
- Engage on social media
- Issue newsletters
- Publish leaders' bulletins
- Conduct conference calls
- Host webinars
- Make personal visits

It's one thing to see a personal recruit develop into a leader of their own team, but it is a much bigger and more important thing to constantly move that person to greater levels of action and results.

My philosophy has always been to *build leaders and teams will come.* Our System is designed for brand-new green recruits with just the existing natural market at their disposal to develop an ever-growing downline team under them, producing constant cash flow overrides.

What does the finished product look like? Licensed RMDs producing business and sales, and leaders who are running their own *RMD Leadership Factories.*

CHAPTER 31

RUN A HERO-MAKING MACHINE

Every human being is hardwired to want to be recognized, rewarded, and emotionally fed. They want to be significant and know that they matter. During my Amway days, I learned that recognition is as important as financial rewards, so I've always made it a point to develop a recognition and promotion system, providing contests where people can fight for rewards, including trips and other awards. I knew that if I helped my team members achieve *their* dreams and receive promotions, my promotions and level of production would follow. In our business, one of the most important abilities is to be a Director of Motivation (DOM). When our leaders inspire their teams to pursue their next promotion or achievement level, it drives their production and cash flow too. One of the basic DOM tools is to have all of your leaders competing daily for their rankings on the leaderboard.

We have always built our businesses from great event to great event. While it's terrific to have energy and momentum at your office every day, your team also has to experience the environment of a big meeting or convention in person. When they feel the energy, see other leaders, hear their successes, and watch award winners get their awards on stage, then they envision themselves getting those awards and being on stage too! Only at big meetings can their vision get stretched on a deep, emotional level. Many times, a plant can only reach its great potential by being repotted. These events are the ultimate tool for a *DOM*. By making the bigger commitment and paying the costs of transporting yourself to one of these great events, you transform yourself into a *greater you*.

I have invested more money in the team motivation side of the business than any other business expense. I can't even calculate the amount of money I've spent over the years on recognition, from hosting huge conventions to footing the bill for awards, plaques, trophies, prizes, videos, travel, hotel accommodations, meals, and so forth. But I promise it has been worth every penny. Recognition is something that feeds a person's soul and is incredibly rewarding.

Most people and businesses get it backwards when they aim for the head first instead of the heart. They limit their possibilities when they focus their recruiting efforts on logic, numbers, and education alone. All of these factors are important, but they won't ignite the passion that comes with being sold a dream, an opportunity, or the prospect of being a part of an enabling environment and cause. If you can capture *that* in a business like financial services, having big teams who generate enormous wealth is highly achievable.

I could always tell who the great leaders were by seeing who followed them to these big events. I learned a long time ago that while it's difficult to stretch your own vision, you can always submit to *something bigger than yourself* that will stretch your vision for you.

During the early days of my railroad career, I was in the *Perspirational Marketing Business,* which quickly became the *Desperational Marketing Business* for me. Finally, I learned the power of the *Inspirational Marketing Business* and have been in that business ever since, while all my competitors remained in the lesser paradigms of just selling insurance or building a linear agency.

Throughout my career I knew that recognizing and rewarding people would inspire them to do great things. I've always viewed myself as a *Kingmaker*. Two stories taught me the importance of lifting others.

The first story involves Grantland Rice, an American sportswriter in the 1920s who was known for his way with words. Rice very consciously set out to make heroes of sports figures who impressed him. In 1921, Babe Ruth, the legendary American baseball player, hit an astonishing fifty-nine home runs. He had already begun putting up amazing numbers but had yet to become the legend we know him as today. It wasn't until Grantland Rice aimed his *Hero-Making Machine* at Babe Ruth that he became a larger-than-life hero.

Grantland wrote about Ruth as being almost superhuman. His columns about the slugger had Americans hanging on every pitch, hit, and home run. As he was elevated in the public eye, Ruth hit sixty home runs in 1927—something that had never been done. Grantland had hyped Babe, but then Babe lived up to the hype. The funny thing is that sixty home runs was only one more than he had hit six years earlier, but no one gave it much note then. The difference? This time, Babe had been immortalized by the hero-making machine of the great Grantland Rice. With the help of one another, both are now in the Hall of Fame.

The second story involves someone almost everyone has heard of: Muhammad Ali. Many consider him the greatest boxer of all time, but that alone is not what made him known to the world. Before he was the outspoken and confident hero we all recognize, he was actually a pretty shy young man who went by the name Cassius Clay. He was a talented boxer who wanted to fill arenas and earn lots of money, but to do that he knew he needed something more.

In 1961, Clay found what that *something more* was. He met a pro wrestler named Gorgeous George while in Las Vegas doing media rounds for their events. It was there that Clay saw Gorgeous George being outlandish, loud, and arrogant. George put on a show for the crowd. Clay knew he needed to do the same. That's when he became the confident character we think of today. Clay said that Gorgeous George told him, "People would come to see me get beat. Others would come to see me win. I'd get 'em coming and going."[12]

Even after developing his bold character, Clay still needed a Hero-Making Machine to hype him up. Enter Howard Cosell. Cosell was a brash, cigar-smoking, American sports journalist with a national broadcast platform who could do for Cassius Clay what Grantland Rice had done decades earlier for Babe Ruth through his syndicated newspaper column. Cosell said of himself, "I've been called arrogant, pompous, obnoxious, vain, cruel, verbose, a showoff. And, of course, I am."[13] By this time Clay had changed his name to Muhammed Ali, and Cosell saw an opportunity with him. He knew that by constantly hyping this now controversial boxer on national television, he would also be hyping himself.

In the 1960s and '70s Cosell covered Ali by calling most of his fights and frequently interviewing him. They complemented each other. Cosell knew he needed the arrogant Ali, and Ali seemed to know he needed the brash Cosell.

So, the message for all you DOMs out there: Just as Rice's Hero-Making Machine elevated Ruth, and Cosell's Hero-Making Machine made a legend out of Ali, so can you help create the new legends of tomorrow by lifting up your team.

CHAPTER 32

PAID TO IMITATE, NOT CREATE

ONCE I FOUND OUT THAT, IN OUR BUSINESS, *YOU'RE PAID TO imitate, not create,* I taught our leaders that those who were fastest to copy my System exactly would achieve the highest success. I warned them that it would probably cost them a million dollars per creative thought, so they should have as many creative thoughts as they could afford. Even though we learned in school that it's bad to copy, we teach that in our world it's just the opposite—copying is not only good, but it's the best way to build your business. One vital secret I've learned is that you are way more likely to get paid if you imitate a successful system instead of creating one.

I talk a lot about formatting and copying, but, of course, you have to make sure the *master copy* is worth duplicating. It does you no good to copy mediocrity. Instead, copy greatness and discipline.

I have always searched for people who would follow the System, but what I was really searching for were leaders who'd copy *more* than a system. I wanted someone who would learn and copy a Recruiter's Mentality *and* a Builder's Mindset. Changing your behavior is important, but when you can change your mentality, your mindset, and your paradigm, then the sky's the limit.

I'm certainly not the first to suggest that you study others and copy their route to success. Industrialist Andrew Carnegie commissioned Napoleon Hill to study the most successful people at the turn of the twentieth century. His research took over two decades and more than five hundred interviews to complete, and it covered titans such as Henry Ford and Thomas Edison. His findings, written in his bestseller *Think and Grow Rich,* included (and I'm paraphrasing), *If you want to become a millionaire, find one and copy exactly what they do.*[14]

Years ago, I was holding a meeting with an up-and-coming team in the Boston area. When the meeting was over, one of our new associates introduced himself and his invited guest—his uncle, who, it turned out, was an esteemed professor at Harvard Business School. Upon hearing that, I was expecting to get a negative response from him, but to my surprise, he was very positive about my business presentation.

When he learned that his nephew was getting involved with a new insurance marketing company, he wanted to check it out. Initially, he thought he might have to save his nephew from some type of business scheme, but once he attended our meeting, he was pleasantly surprised by my message. He told me that I was right when I said most people want to know the best way to go into business and succeed. He said, "Of course, there is the rare person who can start and succeed at business without following the traditional rules of that business, but for the vast majority, I teach them these principles: One, find a business with a proven plan that works. Two, find a business that has mentors who will partner up and coach you along the way. And three, find out if the architect of the system is still in the game." He added, "You know, we charge a lot of money at Harvard to teach our students these principles." It was very validating to be told by one of the best at Harvard Business School that we checked all three of those boxes he teaches to his students.

Copying a millionaire seems like great advice on the surface, but there are a couple of challenges to be aware of. First, it's not always easy to find a millionaire, especially one who's willing to share. And second, what they did to become a millionaire is rarely easy to replicate. You *can't* exactly do what Henry Ford, Thomas Edison, or others like them have done. You can't recreate all the circumstances of their success. And that includes copying modern innovators such as Steve Jobs, Bill Gates, or Elon Musk, because they each have a combination of unique life circumstances, psyches, and other key random factors that simply aren't duplicatable.

It is better to copy a proven system than it is to copy an individual. The founder of McDonald's, Ray Kroc, understood this. He knew that if his company was to become successful, he'd have to address people's tendency to become distracted by their own creativity; he'd have to devise an exact formatted system they could easily follow. His success in building the McDonald's franchises came from his *Business Franchise Format System*. He left nothing to chance. He knew that having a system made things predictable, foolproof, and profitable, so he built a duplicatable system where new franchisee entrepreneurs' chances for success were all but guaranteed.

Think of yourself as a copy machine, then take the next chapters in this book and copy them with cookie-cutter exactness. When someone follows the success principles of my System and then masters them, they become a *Duplicator*, and when they teach others to become a Duplicator by following my System, then they become a *Replicator*. The growth of the business is in the production of Replicators.

I'm going to invite you to copy my System exactly if you're looking for one to build wealth. The key is, find a system that works and copy it. And those who copy the fastest win! Again, there aren't many millionaires—let alone billionaires—offering to tell you exactly what they did to get where they are, but I am. The speed and exactness with which you copy the System will, in large part, determine your success. This cookie-cutter exactness must be duplicated throughout your team.

CHAPTER 33

THEY DIDN'T *DO* BUSINESS AT IBM—THEY *BUILT* ONE

I OWE A LOT OF OUR HISTORIC GROWTH TO CONTINUALLY studying the great leaders and successful business models. I was particularly inspired by how IBM grew into such an industry giant. Because they are a company I've long admired, I adopted many of their success principles. Thomas Watson, the founder of IBM, once attributed his company's phenomenal success to three principles.

The first was that, at the very beginning, he had a very clear picture of what the company would look like when it was finally done—a model in his mind of what it would look like when *the vision* was in place.

The second was that he then created a picture in his mind of how IBM would act when it was finally done.

The third was that, with those two successful pictures in his mind, he then realized that unless the leaders began to act that way from the very beginning, they would never get there.

In other words, he realized that for IBM to become a great company it would have to act like a great company long before it ever became one.

From the very outset, IBM was fashioned after the template of Watson's vision. And every day, they attempted to model the company after that template. At the end of each day, they asked themselves how well they had done, and they discovered the disparity between where they were and where they had committed to be. Then, at the start of the following day, they set out to make up for the difference.

Every day at IBM was a day devoted to business development, not doing business. For this reason, you could say: *They didn't do business at IBM—they* built *one.*[15]

CHAPTER 34

BECOME THE CEO
OF YOUR LIFE

I THINK IT'S VITAL THAT YOU HAVE THE MINDSET OF BECOMING the CEO of your life—and especially of your business life. Most people aren't in control of their lives. Those who command their destiny have a strong understanding of time. They know what time is about—how it can work for or against them—and as a result, they have a deep appreciation for the *now*.

Consider how many hours have passed since you've been reading or listening to this book. How many *nows* have there been? We're in the now, right *now*. Life is just a continuous string of *nows*—that's all it is. How each *now* is spent is a singular choice and can happen consciously, unconsciously, or intentionally. We don't get to go back and retry how we spent the last day, hour, or even minute. With such a precious and limited quantity of *nows*, a CEO must be hyperfocused on any system that takes the guesswork out of how to use time for the greatest outcome. The right system can overcome the many human habits that stand in the way. As the CEO of your life, you will learn how important a system is. You cannot rely on willpower and focus alone.

Regardless of what Little Orphan Annie said about tomorrow in her famous song, I have found that there is no tomorrow. There is only today. When I wake up every day, I find that it's always today. We need to avoid the mañana syndrome. To emphasize this, I give watches and clocks to all of our key leaders with the word *now* written in place of numbers. So, when someone asks them what time it is, they just respond, "It's *Now* o'clock!"

CHAPTER 35

BE A STUDENT OF THE BUSINESS

I KNOW I'VE WRITTEN ABOUT *READY...FIRE...AIM, STUMBLING Forward and Staying Confused*, and *Ignorant Enthusiasm*, but I don't want to give you the impression that you don't have to know anything about your industry. You better believe I became a student of the business, and so did my team. Being in highly regulated industries like insurance and securities, you must know what you're doing so you can act in the best interest of the client. So yes, you should be a student of whatever it is you're trying to accomplish—not just a casual observer or a hobbyist.

What I like about being a student is that students are constantly learning, growing, and expanding. You should never be satisfied or lulled into thinking you've learned enough. As a constant student not only of your business but of human nature and life in general, you will be armed with knowledge that translates into power with your clients and team. So many people get it wrong when becoming a student of the business; they think they have to know everything before they even start. It's actually the reverse. *Knowledge doesn't produce activity— activity produces knowledge.* Probably the most important part of the business a leader needs to focus on is being a student of how to master and run the Leadership Format System. This accomplishes two very important things: First, it builds your business team by continuously opening outlets. And second, it simultaneously moves production through the outlets. It's this repetition of the System and sales activity that hones your skills. *Repetition is the mother of skill.*

You are what you repeatedly think about and then do. The whole concept of following a system is to imbue you with a new set of habits that, if followed, will take you to great success. I have learned that *what flows through you sticks to you*. I love a quote often attributed to the poet Ralph Waldo Emerson, "Sow a thought and you reap an action; sow an act and you reap a habit; sow a habit and you reap a character; sow a character and you reap a destiny."

CHAPTER 36

REPLACE FULL-TIME NIGHTMARES
WITH PART-TIME DREAMS

ONE DAY, ART GATHERED SEVERAL OF THE COMPANY LEADERS together for a picture intended to show the scope of the ALW opportunity. We all dressed in the attire of our former careers to illustrate that people from all walks of life could succeed at ALW. We had doctors, athletes, stay-at-home moms, pilots, lawyers, and more. I dressed in my old railroad clothes—a plaid shirt, jeans, boots, railroad hat, and my old lantern. We were asked to give a quote that would inspire others to join, and I came up with a saying that still embraces what I'm doing today: "I replace full-time nightmares with part-time dreams." This became an unofficial motto for the entire company.

The sentiment summed up the way I had felt during my railroad career—my full-time nightmare—and how I felt when I found ALW—my part-time dream. Decades later, I find this philosophy as true as it's ever been. Human nature hasn't changed since I started at ALW. People still dream; they still want to be somebody. They are tired of their current situation and often feel trapped. If you can provide a vehicle to help them escape their nightmares and turn their dreams into reality, then you have found one of the great secrets to building a successful business.

I always taught my leaders, if you are trying to be the best vacuum cleaner salesperson, you had better bring a good vacuum cleaner with you. It better work when you plug it in, and it better clean when you're demonstrating it to the customer. The same is true in our business. *It's hard to sell a dream if you're dragging a nightmare to the door. You'd better bring your dream demonstrator with you.*

CHAPTER 37

THE POWER OF MOZONE

I ALWAYS LOVED THE OLD TV SHOW *THE TWILIGHT ZONE*. THE show started with the narrator, Rod Serling, saying, "You're traveling through another dimension, a dimension not only of sight and sound but of mind. A journey into a wondrous land whose boundaries are that of imagination. That's the signpost up ahead—your next stop, the Twilight Zone!"[16] That always captured my imagination. When we started building the business, we created something called the *Mozone*. I knew that people had to *feel* and *experience* the opportunity as much as they had to learn about it.

Mozone is short for *Momentum Zone*. I wanted it to be like another dimension people entered as they came into the presence of one of our leaders, into one of our offices, or into one of our event centers. You recruit people into an environment and atmosphere, not just into a company. Mozone is what runs the *Dream-Selling Machine* that creates an exciting, quality, professional recruiting environment and capitalizes on the Magic of Crowds and synergy.

The more meeting attendees there are, the greater the sense of urgency to get in and get started. The excitement and enthusiasm becomes contagious. The success of your meetings will be dictated by the size of your crowds. It's hard to give a bad presentation or have a bad meeting when there is anticipation in the air and a buzz of success all around.

Mozone is affected by everything you do: how you dress, how you talk, how you walk, how you stand, how you smile, and so on. If you're not smiling, if you're negative, if your body language stinks, if you're talking softly, then you are sliding into the *SLOWzone* and even possibly the *NOzone*. If you normally walk slowly, then walk faster. If you normally talk slowly, then talk faster and louder. Smile more. Stand up straighter. And bring the energy. You are an influencing machine for good or bad—make sure it's for the good.

People won't make a conversion in their lives unless they go through some bigger emotional experience. I never once recruited anyone with data, a spreadsheet, or logic. It was the Mozone that attracted them and subsequently converted them.

Everything in life is influenced by these two words: *FEEL* and *NOW*. It's how you *feel now* that counts—not how you used to feel or how you hope to feel in the future. Our meetings, while packed with great information, are designed to help people feel hope. To quote Abraham Lincoln, "When I do good I feel good, when I do bad, I feel bad…"[17] Another way of saying that is, *It's not what people* know, *it's how they* feel *that counts.* When they come through our doors, instead of just using *mind thinking*, we ignite their *heart thinking*, emotionalizing them to feel what we are trying to teach them. Before they leave, they're motivated to *do good*. Remember, as it says in Proverbs, "As he thinketh in his heart, so is he" (23:7 KJV). It's plain to me that our Heavenly Father wants us to think with our hearts more than with our minds. Only then will people be ready to accept all of the magical simplifications before which all resistance crumbles. I didn't join ALW or start WMA or HGI because of logic. It was because I switched off my thinking process and became *converted*. It was because I *felt* part of a new idea and crusade. When people think too much, they suffer from analysis paralysis or what I call *stinking thinking*. (Just remember how this is spelled: *analysis*.)

I learned about the power of big meetings from my Amway days. I remember absorbing, like a sponge, the inspirational and powerful building techniques that changed my life forever. I also remember getting my first recognition and being able to speak at those early rallies. What an impact that had on my life! As I look back on my career, those big events set the stage for the success that was to come.

I will never forget the impression my first *Fast Start School* (a two-day motivational and training meeting designed for new recruits) made on me during my early ALW days. It was held in Atlanta, at the old Admiral Benbow Inn. I could tell from the moment I walked in that all the experience I'd gained from attending those big Amway motivational meetings would somehow enable me to transform ALW into the Amway of the insurance industry.

It would be hard to imagine my career without Fast Start–type schools and conventions. They remain one of the great, unique aspects of our company today and will always perpetuate our incredible growth.

Reality is the enemy of dreams. When someone comes to one of our meetings, or if we talk to them individually, it is highly likely life has kicked them in the teeth. Their confidence is low, they've suffered economic setbacks, and they are concerned about the future, so the last thing they need is another dose of reality. They need someone to sell them a dream. If you just talk to people about reality, no one will follow you. If I chose to just sell insurance instead of dreams, then no one would have followed me. My job is to free people from their ties to mediocrity and unite them with a new community of successful and energetic people.

A principle I learned from Eric Hoffer's book *The True Believer: Thoughts on the Nature of Mass Movements* is that the following two things have to occur simultaneously for an important movement to take hold: First, there has to be a very high degree of dissatisfaction among the people you're recruiting. Second, there must be leaders who are prepared for that moment and who can step into the void and take charge.[18] I had caught a glimpse of this in Amway. There was a growing dissatisfaction with the way things were going in America in the late 1970s. Having a job wasn't enough anymore; people were looking for more.

By the time we were starting ALW, the degree of dissatisfaction in the country had grown, largely because of the recession, rising unemployment, and inflation. When I saw how big the insurance problem was nationwide and the common-sense solution Buy Term and Invest the Difference spreading like wildfire, I knew that we had everything needed for this to be the great solution to this problem. Art had only one part of the solution: the crusade (the warhead)—and I had the other part of the solution: the System (the missile), to deliver his crusade to the masses.

CHAPTER 38

THE ULTIMATE DRIVEN, DETERMINED DREAMERS: THE MONTE AND LISA HOLM STORY

EARLIER I TOLD YOU ABOUT GLENN MILLS' UNLIKELY BUSINESS startup in Raleigh, North Carolina. What I'd like to share now is a great example of how the System brought the cream to the top. Glenn had been holding his weekly Opportunity Meetings, and a young man named Monte Holm attended one of them. Monte was a fresh-faced twenty-year-old who was nearing the end of his two-year, full-time mission for our church, The Church of Jesus Christ of Latter-day Saints. Monte had heard so much about this business opportunity from one of Glenn's downline leaders, Bob Dooley (also a local church member), that soon Monte was hooked. He loved what he was hearing and decided this was the career direction he wanted to take when he finished his mission and headed back to St. George, Utah, a few weeks later.

Remember, while all of this was happening, I had already moved to Denver and launched our new business. One day, out of the blue, I got a call from Bob Dooley in Raleigh, telling me about this young returning missionary named Monte Holm who was determined to join the ALW business. After two or three conversations, Bob finally convinced me that it would be worth my time to talk to Monte. I had been putting it off because Monte didn't exactly fit the mold of what we were looking for. Young and single wasn't the ideal prospect profile—mid-thirties, married, with a family was more like it—but Monte was persistent and wouldn't take no for an answer.

I finally reached out and challenged him to set up an Opportunity Meeting in St. George, where I expected him to gather about thirty good recruit prospects. The flight to St. George was a rough one with lots of turbulence, giving me a mild case of vertigo. After landing, I took some time to recover from my SkyWest (or as I called it, *ScareWest*) flight, and then we got to work. Monte had booked an old, theater-type room for the meeting. The place looked like it hadn't been used in years, so we cleaned the cobwebs, swept the floors, and dusted off the chairs, tables, and anything else that needed a wipe-down.

I was curious to see what caliber of people were going to show up. When the time came to start, a stream of middle-aged, gray-haired men, all sharply dressed, poured in. They loved Monte and were eager to listen. The meeting was a great success. People were excited. We did several policy analyses and recruited some wonderful folks.

I told Monte that as a young, single guy, until he got married he wasn't going to have any roots. A few months later he called to tell me that he was engaged to his sweetheart, Lisa. Even though Monte was young, he knew how to make things happen.

Monte called a few months later, excited to tell me about his great new recruits and to say that he really wanted me to see his new office. New office? I didn't know anything about a new office, and I especially didn't know that it was in Las Vegas. Monte had moved from St. George to Vegas and was quickly off to a successful start. I immediately flew over to meet his new leaders.

These new recruits were the kind of guys I had been hoping he would bring into the business. They were the kind that took initiative and had the Ready . . . Fire . . . Aim mentality. Monte became a great leader at ALW. Keep in mind that it all started because **Glenn Mills**, in **Macon, Georgia**, refused to give up, then went to **Raleigh**, where he found his success, and all of that led to one of my first superstars in **Monte**. That chain of events changed thousands of lives. The System has a way of taking young, excited men and women and compensating for what they don't know. It saved Glenn from himself and it made Monte bigger than himself. The System brings the cream to the top, and that was Monte, my first great Driven, Determined Dreamer.

Things were happening so fast that I couldn't help but think there was a Divine hand in it all. I wanted to be somebody and wanted to help others with their dreams, and that's exactly what was happening. Things were being placed in my path—*glorious accidents*—and it was up to me to recognize them and act upon them. Now you see why it's so important to never ignore an ambitious person, regardless of their circumstances. My job was to recruit and provide an opportunity, not to judge people before they ever had a chance to try.

Recruit everyone you can. Every person has the seed of greatness in them. For most it lies dormant under the surface. It's our great opportunity to become the dream activators. I could have easily skipped taking two days from my schedule to travel to St. George. But I'm glad I didn't. Don't be too hasty judging people in advance. The System filters through a lot of people who do a little bit to help us progress, and eventually it identifies the future stars. Monte built an incredible national team. He would go on to attract and train leaders and send them all across the nation to open offices, much like I had done. He was our first truly national Super Team builder.

Remember, *it only takes a small spark to ignite a great future.*

CHAPTER 39

LOTS OF PEOPLE DOING A LITTLE, AND A FEW DOING A LOT

THIS PRINCIPLE IS ABOUT USING THE *LAW OF HIGH NUMBERS* TO make the Law of Averages profitable. The Law of Averages is a simple concept; it says that after doing a task repeatedly, you will finally settle on averages of outcome. In our business, that means coming to know the average amount of invites it takes for you to get someone to attend a meeting or meet with you in person. Or the average number of attendees who will join the company and how many, on average, will then become a client, and in turn become a leader, and so on.

This is the key to the enormous success of all of the great companies we have built. If you're going to stay small, you don't need a system, but if you're going to go from average or ordinary numbers to high or extraordinary numbers, you need a vehicle like our Leadership Format System to take you there. Remember that by applying the *Law of High Numbers* to the Law of Averages, you will ultimately build a great team of *Lots of People Doing a Little Bit, and a Few Doing a Lot.*

CHAPTER 40

I HAD A SECRET THAT WAS GOING TO CHANGE THE WORLD

EVER SINCE I JOINED ALW AND REALIZED THAT MY LEADERSHIP Format System would be the key to disrupting the entire insurance industry, changing the insurance-buying habits of Middle America, I have awakened each morning with the tremendously powerful feeling that I was in possession of a secret success formula that no one else in the world fully understood. It was the feeling that I could do something better than the billions of other people on this planet. My formula is ideal for building a tremendously viral distribution system able to market complex products like life insurance, mutual funds, annuities, and more. Part of my mission is to share this secret with as many people as I can. My secret has always been easily transferable and duplicatable.

The System is so viral that as I taught it to all of the top leaders at ALW, it spread like wildfire throughout the company even though many didn't fully understand the psychology of it. I was selling dreams, opportunities, and concepts, while everyone else was mostly focused on selling insurance. They were educating people on the nature of the product while I was building enthusiasm around the possibility of the dream. Which do you think people wanted? Of course, the answer is *the dream*. That was how we built an empire.

While most others were focusing more on product knowledge, I was using a contagious psychology. My viral enthusiasm about the opportunity infected our team. I taught my System leaders that by first aiming at the prospect's heart, their head would follow. Essentially, by appealing to their dreams, sales of our product were inevitable. We sold to those we recruited, and we sold to those who didn't join.

Our leaders understood this vital principle: *Set yourself on fire with enthusiasm and when the crowd gathers to watch you burn, recruit them.* Recruiting them means teaching them concepts that change their lives for the better. In this way, we are benefitting them and not just selling to them—we are giving them tools and principles they can use to enhance their lives.

My concept of Friendship Borrowing solved the age-old prospecting problem that the industry faced. For example, if I knew Prospect A for six months and he referred me to Prospect B, whom he had known for five years, that meant I had known Prospect B for five years and six months too. I borrowed Prospect A's five years. It's the concurrent linking up of relationships. The traditional industry was built more on cold calling and purchasing leads. But we focused on recruiting and selling to warm markets. While most of the industry just aimed for sales, we aimed for warm referrals who became profit centers as well as clients.

CHAPTER 41

THE TEAM WITH THE MOST OUTLETS WINS

THE RAPID, RELENTLESS, REPETITION OF THE SIX SIMPLE STEPS OF MY Leadership Format System led to the continuous opening of outlets (the signing of new recruits) and the simultaneous movement of production through those outlets (the selling of products). This is the Rosetta Stone for building an empire. I was continuously opening outlets and selling products. I always challenged my team to *run the System and let the System sort the leaders out and create the production.*

If the System is run correctly, each new recruit should yield a minimum of four sales—one internal consumption/system sale to the new recruit, and three sales to their trainees. This is done by having a *Field Trainer* take them through the Six System Steps and Eight Speed Filters, to recruit and make internal consumption sales to them and their three top prospects. Each new recruit watches and learns as their most promising prospects are introduced to the opportunity through the skillful approach of an established leader. Then the System causes this process to be repeated again and again with each new recruit.

If you want to sell more products, you need more outlets (places to sell your product). McDonald's sells more hamburgers than any other restaurant in the world because they have more locations—more outlets. Coca-Cola sells more soft drinks than any other brand because there are more places to buy a Coke. Pretty simple. If I wanted to be number one and sell more insurance, I simply needed to have more outlets to move my product than anyone else. Distribution is king, and whoever has the most outlets wins.

Remember, it is a race for outlets, and the starting gun has already sounded!

CHAPTER 42

AN IMPERFECT PLAN
VIOLENTLY EXECUTED

FOR THE FIRST THREE MONTHS IN DENVER, WE WERE HOLDING meetings in a little hotel because I hadn't opened an office yet. At church during my first week, I met a member who was the assistant manager of this hotel. He gave me a great deal that allowed me to have our meetings on Tuesday and Thursday nights, and Saturday mornings.

I remembered Art's motto: *Just do it* (he used that long before Nike adopted it). So many people wait for conditions to be perfect before they get to work. Not me. I was singularly focused on recruiting people from all walks of life and was confident our System would sort out those who had developed a Recruiter's Mentality and a Builder's Mindset. Given my experience at Amway, building through in-home opportunity meetings, I knew that I didn't have to have an office to create my team. The office would have to come later.

We met in the hotel for a while until another opportunity presented itself. At the top of my prospect list was Roy Cox, a friend from Macon who had just moved to Denver after retiring from the military. I reached out to recruit him and discovered he was a property manager at an office complex nearby! I told Roy that in the near future I would be ready to rent some office space. He agreed to let me use one of their conference rooms until the time was right. But then he had a better idea. He sent me to see their meeting scheduler and approved for me to utilize some of the vacant conference rooms for the three times a week I held my meetings. I suddenly had access to any conference room that was available, allowing us to keep growing until we finally leased our first office from him. By the way...I ended up recruiting Roy. Waiting until conditions are perfect to pull the trigger is a recipe for failure.

CHAPTER 43

WHEN IN DOUBT, HOLD A MEETING— EVEN IF NO ONE COMES

A LONG TIME AGO, I LEARNED A SUREFIRE CURE FOR ANYTHING that ailed people in our business: Simply *hold a meeting*! It doesn't matter where or with whom; if you hold a meeting, good things tend to happen. If you get a bunch of noes, *hold a meeting*! If sales don't close, *hold a meeting*! If you get stood up, *hold a meeting*! If times get tough, *hold a meeting*! You probably get the idea. Great things are just a meeting away, so the most important meeting you'll ever hold is the next one!

The first Opportunity Meeting I ever held in California is proof of this very idea. One weekend, Nate Knowles had come from San Jose to visit us. He was a retired military friend of Dick Rainwater's, one of my new star leaders in Denver. Even though Nate only came to Denver to visit his friend, Dick brought him to one of our Opportunity Meetings. As a result, Nate became intrigued and told us that he was interested in starting with us in California. Since we didn't have outlets there yet, I told him that I would let him know if and when that possibility presented itself.

Dick pulled me aside a couple of weeks later to tell me that Nate had been excitedly talking to people in California. He already had eight or nine recruits eager to sign up and meet me. I told Dick to hold Nate off for a while until the time was right. But Nate was persistent. I finally told him I would come to San Jose to help him get started. So just as I had done with some of

my other expansion leaders, I coached him on what to say and
what not to say and told him to get thirty prospects together;
rent a meeting room; have a projector, a screen, a chalkboard,
a table, and some chairs available; and I would come.

To be honest, I was excited about the trip because it was my
first time in California. Nate met me at the airport, and we
headed over to the hotel room he had set up. The meeting was
scheduled to start at 7:00 p.m., but as the time approached, no
one had come yet. Nate got a little nervous and uncomfortable.
Well, 7:15 rolled around and still no one had arrived. We had
set up the projector and screen and were waiting. When it was
7:30 and still no one had showed, Nate broke down and cried.
He was incredibly embarrassed and hurt. It was my job to put
on my best leadership hat and help him through this awkward
situation. I offered him some positive words and we tried to
find a silver lining in the situation, but after it was painfully
clear that no one was coming, we finally gathered our supplies
and prepared to go down to the hotel restaurant to grab a bite,
regroup, and talk things over. I made sure he knew I would still
be in town the next day and we would go see those who hadn't
shown up.

Just as we left the meeting room and were walking to the
restaurant, one of his invited prospects came running down
the hall in a hurry to get to the meeting. After he apologized
for being late, Nate almost told him that no one had showed
up, but I jumped in and, instead of dwelling on the negative,
told him that he'd missed a great meeting, and he would not
believe the story we had to tell. We invited him to join us for
dinner, where I gave him a one-on-one summary of what he'd
missed. This gentleman ended up joining the business and
became Nate's first recruit. To this day he probably still has

no idea that no one else showed up at that first meeting. You never know what will come from your next meeting—even when nobody shows up! So, when in doubt, just *hold a meeting!*

What kind of meetings? One-on-One Meetings, Home Opportunity Meetings, Online Meetings, Business Opportunity Meetings at the prospect's office, and Super Team Meetings. And don't forget about meetings at Leadership Format School, Top Gun School, RMD Academies, Company Conventions, and International Super Trips.

From small to big, there are many types of meetings. I have always built my businesses from meeting to meeting and from great event to great event. Just as creeks and streams feed into small rivers and small rivers feed into bigger rivers, which ultimately feed into oceans, our smallest meetings ultimately feed into our great super conventions.

There have been times when the power went out and I held a meeting in complete darkness. When the lights finally came back on, I was amazed to see that no one had left. Once I even held a meeting next door to a Hell's Angels party, where I had to shout my entire presentation so loud that I lost my voice. I have given meetings in the back of Jack Linder's Purina feed-store where the smell was *awful*. There were even a couple of rats running across my feet while I presented. Later Jack told me that the rats had grown so big by eating the cattle feed and he had even given them a nickname. I was amazed everyone stayed, but they did.

The first Amway meeting I held was to sell the dream to my next-door neighbor; we sat at their kitchen table. I held my first ALW meeting while riding sixty miles per hour on the caboose of a 150-car freight train at 2:00 a.m. I drew out the business plan for my new flagman by the light of our lanterns on the back of a cardboard box. That little meeting on the back of a train eventually led to ALW's last big meeting before its merger—a gathering of 35,000 people at the Super Dome in New Orleans in 1988.

Ten years later, in my next venture at WMA, we had 27,500 associates at the MGM Grand Hotel and Resort in Las Vegas. As you can see, one of my greatest secrets to success has indeed been to *hold a meeting*! As I've said before, I have always been able to identify my great leaders by seeing how many other leaders followed them to such events.

CHAPTER 44

NEVER LOSE MOMENTUM—EVEN UNDER A CEASE AND DESIST ORDER

WHILE I WAS ON ONE OF MY EARLY CALIFORNIA START-UP TRIPS with Nate Knowles, I called my Denver office to check in. My secretary answered and excitedly told me, "Hubert! Chip and Bill have to talk to you. Oh, it's serious! You're not going to believe it!"

I asked what was going on, but all she could do was repeat what she had just said. I knew this couldn't be good.

Chip Taylor and Bill McCord were running the meetings in Denver for me while I was on the road opening up California. I found out that they had recruited the Colorado insurance commissioner's son-in-law. There was nothing wrong with that. The problem arose when, for several weeks during their Opportunity Meetings, they introduced him to the crowd, seemingly implying that we had the endorsement of the insurance commissioner.

When my secretary finally got Chip on the phone, he told me that the chief investigator for the Colorado Department of Insurance had come by and issued a cease and desist order. I couldn't believe it. Why on earth would they do that? They read me the letter and, sure enough, we were told to halt all operations. I would have to have a meeting with the commissioner when I returned.

I was baffled by this. As far as I knew, we were operating properly. Our business was a juggernaut, and we were growing like crazy. Nothing was going to stop that momentum—not even an unwarranted cease and desist order from the Colorado Insurance Commissioner.

Chip and Bill seemed equally mystified and didn't offer any possible explanations. They especially didn't volunteer any information about the commissioner's son-in-law being acknowledged at ALW meetings. I called our legal counsel, Kevin King, back in Atlanta, explained what I knew of the situation, and asked for the company's support. Kevin said that I was on my own, but that I should meet with the commissioner and report back.

I didn't know which was more shocking—receiving a cease and desist order from the commissioner or finding out that I was going to have to play the role of the company attorney. It wasn't like I was some small recruit in a remote state doing a tiny amount of business. I was the biggest guy in the company!

When I met with the commissioner, I walked in having no idea what any of this was about. Ironically, the commissioner and I were members of the same church, so I hoped that would secure me a little mercy for whatever situation had arisen. Boy, was I wrong! This guy wasn't messing around. He let me talk for a while, so I explained what we were doing, and I assured him that our advertisements were properly representing our products. I was stating my innocence when all of a sudden he startled me with a quote from Shakespeare's *Hamlet*: "Me thinks thou doth protest too much."[19]

Then he had his assistant bring in five or six big boxes filled with flyers and brochures that Chip and Bill had put together in my absence. The flyers highlighted the Buy Term and Invest the Difference concept encouraging the replacement of traditional cash value, whole life insurance policies. The flyers didn't have any kind of disclaimers or disclosures. We had rocked the commissioner's world because he had spent his whole career in the traditional whole life industry. He was especially miffed because we had stirred up a hornet's nest of upset insurance agents who were demanding that he stop us from replacing their policies. He finally brought up how his son-in-law was being held up at our meetings as a tacit endorsement of our company.

Finally, I had a pretty good sense of why he was upset. After seeing this for the first time, I knew Chip and Bill, in their enthusiasm, were to blame. I had been trying to convince him that we were doing everything correctly, only to have him bring out boxes of damaging evidence.

I worked a bit of my story into our discussion, and I think the fact that I had been a bishop for a congregation in Macon helped calm him down. He had never seen a business model like ours and was being bombarded from all sides. Competing agents, clients, and other insurance companies were complaining about our new company. What's more, we had put in applications for five hundred agents to be appointed with the state—more people than had applied in the prior *five years*! We were on their radar, so we needed to behave.

After he put a good scare in me, I convinced him that I didn't know anything about the flyers and that I would work hard to correct the problem and rein in any offenders. He agreed to cancel the cease and desist order.

So what's the point of this story?

During the cease and desist, we didn't slow down at all. This is why leadership and vision are so important. While this would have stopped weaker teams, we didn't let it kill any of our momentum. I wasn't taking my foot off the gas. We kept running our Tuesday, Thursday, and Saturday Opportunity and Recruiting Meetings. During those fourteen days under the order, I told the team to take the ALW sign down and put up a MILICO sign instead (the name of our insurance company). The slogan for the meetings was "Go, Go, Go with MILICO," and none of the literature mentioned me or ALW. During this time, we recruited 150 people and kept building our business!

Now, I'm not a lawyer and in no way am I advocating that you break the law or ignore it. I'm just telling you that unforeseen events will always pop up. Some might be small, and some might be big enough to put you down if you let them. Protect the momentum you have and fight like crazy to never lose it.

CHAPTER 45

RELENTLESSLY DUPLICATE THE MASTER COPY: THE RICH AND CINDY THAWLEY STORY

As Nate's team began to grow, I sent him a VHS tape of me giving an Opportunity presentation. I intended for him to share it with the new team members he was training. As Nate was Taprooting down one of his new legs (essentially coaching and mentoring a group of new downline team members), about six or seven people deep, one of his new recruits, Bill, led Nate to a young newlywed couple, Rich and Cindy Thawley, who would eventually become some of the all-time greats in the industry.

This is a typical example of how viral and organic our System is. Bill was a musician who had performed at Rich and Cindy's wedding a few months earlier, so it was natural for him to share our concepts with these newlyweds. He explained that for a young married couple, the concept of Buy Term and Invest the Difference was much more valuable at their stage of life than traditional life insurance. As Bill was leaving, he casually mentioned to Rich that his manager was possibly hiring. Rich was intrigued, and a few days later he went to Nate's office where he learned about this exciting new business opportunity. Nate and Bill explained it all to him and showed him my video presentation, which led to Rich joining the company.

Rich reminded me of a young Tom Cruise. He was a good-looking, ambitious young guy who wanted more out of life. He worked for San Jose State University, making around $18,000 a year, and his wife worked as a substitute teacher. Rich had an additional part-time job shoveling horse manure for his father's commercial landscaping company. Needless to say, Rich knew there were better opportunities out there to make more money. He was ready.

I had told Nate to call me if he ever had a live one on the line and I'd help reel him in. After Nate told Rich my story, including the fact that I had made over $500,000 in my first year and a half, Rich called me to make sure I was for real and to learn how I did it. When we talked, Rich fell in love with the idea that I had succeeded because of a system. I told him that in the same way McDonald's founder Ray Kroc had developed the Business Franchise Format System for his restaurants, I had developed a duplicatable System for team-building in the insurance world. I let Rich know that if a railroad conductor like me could do this, then I was sure a dynamic person like him could.

Rich wanted to know what was next and when we could meet again. I told him I'd be returning to California in a few weeks, and he should put together a prospect list and start setting up appointments in the interim. On my next trip, Rich and I played golf together, where we talked about business and got to know one another. From that point on, Rich and I talked just about every day for the next eight or nine years.

Rich was like a sponge, absorbing everything he could about knowledge and leadership. He was very particular about who he wanted teaching him. Once he saw that the Master Copy (me) was worth duplicating, he relentlessly copied what I was doing. He became an almost perfect System clone of me, determined to master and implement the tool I had created. He always wanted feedback from me. We would monitor his results, correct whatever needed to be corrected, and move forward. Rich was the guy who had most perfectly copied my mindset and the Leadership Format System process.

Once he saw how the System could help him rapidly ascend the promotion and earnings ladder, he never looked back, becoming a multimillionaire in the process.

The higher up the mountain he ascended, the more he sought my counsel as someone who had already scaled the same peak. He was hungry and focused, and when we would talk, we had a motto: *No slack*. His strength was in his discipline. He was accountable, not only to me but to the System. Rich perfectly exemplified one of my all-time success principles: *The first principle of leadership is followership*. He was paid to *imitate*, not *create*. Soon he was a force to be reckoned with in the great ALW company.

I had found a disciple, my number one guy—someone who was going to work as hard as I was. He wanted to win as much as I did and became a role model for our leaders all across the nation. Rich and Cindy became lifelong friends of mine and Norma's. Rich was one of the most important recruits not only in my life but also in the history of financial services.

Remember, *it only takes a small spark to ignite a great future*.

CHAPTER 46

A MOST IMPROBABLE SUCCESS JOURNEY: THE XUAN NGUYEN STORY

As TIME WENT ON, OTHER LEADERS I MENTORED FOLLOWED Rich's rise to the top. Monte Holm, Jack Linder, Bryce Peterson, and Jeff Miles were among them. They not only ran the System, they caught the vision and duplicated the Recruiter's Mentality and Builder's Mindset I had been preaching. They also developed the Alexander complex and turned the improbable into the inevitable. But there's no more improbable success story than that of Xuan Nguyen, a former social worker with Vietnamese refugees in Northern California.

Global events often create unintended windows of opportunity. At the end of the Vietnam War, many people escaped from Vietnam, and Xuan was among them. As a teenager, he and his family lived in refugee camps, finally settling in San Jose, California. He married his wife, Hoa, and started his career as a social worker. This paid little, so to make extra money, Xuan spent his weekends as a street artist, drawing portraits.

One day, Cheryl Bartlett, one of Rich's new RVPs at ALW, met Xuan when he entered her office by mistake while looking for the new social services location. Through an associate, who also spoke Vietnamese, Cheryl was able to sell the dream to Xuan and recruit him into the company.

Xuan and Hoa immediately started inviting and recruiting others in their community. Soon, they had hundreds of people on their team. All of this happened as he was working to get licensed. Even though he couldn't sell insurance at first, he did the most important thing: He sold the dream! It took Xuan about a year to finally get his insurance license, but all the while his team continued to grow. Once licensed, he was already in a six-figure overriding position. This remarkable success story illustrates how everybody you meet has great potential just waiting to be unleashed.

Even though we were experiencing exciting new growth since we'd opened in California, a whole new era began when Xuan joined the business. The Asian community was primed for our opportunity, and the wave continued to gain momentum. Xuan immediately mastered the Leadership Format System and built a fifty-thousand-person team, which positioned him for great future success. These transformative years at ALW prepared him to be one of the founding members in our next great venture, WMA (now known as World Financial Group, WFG, after its sale to Aegon). Xuan became one of the all-time success stories in financial services history, breaking and setting records—and continues today as an industry icon at WFG.

Once again, I remind you that *it only takes a small spark to ignite a great future*.

CHAPTER 47

MORE "GLORIOUS ACCIDENTS!"

AT ONE POINT, ART HAD PLANNED A LEADERSHIP MEETING TO BE held in Park City, Utah. Chip found out that a friend of ours from our church in Macon, Ron Hadley, recently had been transferred to Salt Lake City by his company, American Family Life Assurance Company (Aflac). Chip called Ron and told him how excited he was about the success we were having with this new venture. Chip was a great hype man, for sure, and told Ron that he *had* to meet with me when I came out to Park City. Unfortunately, Ron was busy on the days I planned to be there, so he didn't think he'd be able to connect with me on this trip.

On the day I arrived in Park City, Ron saw a friend he knew from church, Mark Redman, a disability insurance agent, driving down the road. He flagged him down and convinced him to check out this new company he had just heard about. Since Mark was on the lookout for a better opportunity, he agreed to rearrange his schedule and head to Park City to meet me. Later Mark told us that whenever he headed to work, he would always take a certain route to his office. But on *that* day he pulled out of the driveway and went a completely different way. That was the day that Ron flagged him down. Talk about a *glorious accident!*

In Park City, Mark waited around the hotel hoping to meet me—a guy he had just heard about earlier that day. When we broke for dinner, someone approached and told me that a man was hoping to talk with me. When I met Mark, he explained how he was flagged down by Ron Hadley, who told him to come to this location to discuss a potential business opportunity. It took me a minute to figure out that Chip had contacted our mutual church friend, Ron, who had recently moved to Utah from Georgia, and was the one who had sent Mark to meet me.

Mark loved what he'd heard from Ron, and he joined the business right away. I extended my trip for a few days because Mark wanted to take me around to meet some people. This is what I love about people like Mark. They make quick decisions and act on them right away. The first recruit he arranged for us to meet was his agency boss, Bryce Peterson, who went on to become a great star in our companies. Because there was so much happening in the business at the time, I had to return home to regroup and plan. After all, I had just accidentally opened a new city!

I came back a week later to teach, train, and recruit, and that's when things really took off in Utah. As we unleashed our dream-selling, team-building business System, the Salt Lake City team exploded. There was a multiplying effect, with more and more people joining because we were selling dreams, concepts, and opportunities. We were striking a chord with people—a chord that excited them so much that they shared news of us with others. Remember, many of these people weren't licensed or trained in the life insurance side of the business yet. From this simple twist of fate, a number of future great ALW leaders emerged, among them Jeff Miles, Bryce Peterson, and many others.

Dare I repeat the lesson here again? Yes! *It only takes a small spark to ignite a great future.*

CHAPTER 48

TEAM OVERRIDES ARE THE BEST DISABILITY INCOME PLAN EVER: THE JEFF AND DEBBIE MILES STORY

MARK AND BRYCE HAD SOME PEOPLE LINED UP WHO WERE READY for a great opportunity. One of their first recruits was Max Simpson, an institute religion teacher associated with a local college in Ogden, Utah, and also a part-time insurance salesman. Max didn't waste any time taking me to see his prospects. His first meeting was at a restaurant where twenty-five people packed the reserved room. It was at this meeting that I first met Jeff Miles, who would soon become one of the giants at ALW. He was a student in Max's class who had recently married and been working construction in his father's company. After he injured himself falling off a roof, Jeff became a prime candidate for a new opportunity. He latched on to me and immediately caught the vision, grasped the great possibilities our System represented, and learned everything he could to get off to a fast start. It's important to note that Jeff had incredible support at home from his amazing wife, Debbie. There was no Jeff without Debbie.

Why bother telling you about all of these people you don't know? To show you how quickly things happened in the early days of my business. To show you what can happen when you are *all in* on a crusade. To show you that you don't have to be an expert in a field to start. Many of these people weren't licensed yet, nor were they knowledgeable in the insurance world on their first day. I also tell you this to show you how contagious enthusiasm is—and how it covers a multitude of insecurities. To show you how great things can happen when you surround yourself with the right kind of people. Again, I was able to help recruit all of these people because I was selling the dream instead of just selling insurance. Chip would have never called Ron Hadley. Ron would have never tracked down Mark Redman in the middle of the road. Mark would have never introduced me to Bryce Peterson. Max Simpson would have never joined or filled a restaurant with excited people who were looking to better their lives. And I would have never met Jeff Miles. This happened over and over again in city after city. After about eighteen months with us, Jeff and Debbie moved to Fresno to help open California.

Let me give you a powerful example of why building a business you can override is the most predictable and profitable kind of business. One day while Jeff was up in Sacramento opening an expansion office, he was driving to a field training appointment with one of his leaders. They were on the freeway in heavy California traffic when they saw an injured dog on the road. Jeff's recruit was a dog lover and convinced Jeff to pull over so he could help the animal. Against his better judgment, Jeff parked on the shoulder. His recruit got out of the car on that busy freeway and ran over to help the struggling dog. When he reached down to check on the animal, it panicked and bit his hand. Jeff hopped out of the car and ran to help.

Tragically, all three of them were hit by an oncoming vehicle going sixty miles per hour. Jeff was knocked one hundred feet in the air off the freeway, but his recruit and the dog were killed instantly. Jeff was left unconscious and suffered a severe injury to his knee that almost cost him his leg. He was taken to the hospital where he underwent multiple surgeries that resulted in a year-long rehab. This, of course, sidelined him from walking for quite some time.

While all of this was happening to Jeff, his wife, Debbie, experienced complications with her pregnancy and had to spend time in the hospital as well. Their family was in a tremendous predicament with Jeff laid up for a year and Debbie on bed rest for the last four months of her pregnancy. Needless to say, Jeff was not able to do much with his business, but because he had developed strong leaders who were running our System, his financial situation actually *improved* during this time. This is where running a team-building business that you can override proves to be an invaluable asset. When Jeff was injured, his annual income was around $100,000. Even though he wasn't able to work over the next year, his income grew to $500,000 a year! This is the best example I can imagine of the strength our opportunity affords people.

Jeff and Debbie soon recovered and got back on their feet. They became some of our greatest friends, and Jeff went on to become a tremendous *Warrior General* in our business. He was one of my main wingmen and was instrumental in building the success of ALW *and* WMA.

Mark, Bryce, and Max also became special friends and great leaders at ALW and at my next company—all because I sold them a dream instead of insurance. I'll never forget that while they all ended up buying insurance, they became something much more important than just clients.

CHAPTER 49

BUILDING YOUR TEAM TO LAST

DURING MY TIME IN DENVER, BOE ADAMS BROUGHT A MAN named Dennis Richardson into the company. Dennis, who was from Houston, had a powerful background as a Diamond Direct at Amway (how ironic, considering Art's attitude toward that company) and as a Master General Agent with National Home Life. He was the perfect combination of a big insurance guy and a network marketer. Tall, good-looking, with nice suits and nice cars, he was way fancier than Art could stand. He didn't fit the part-time, greenie mold Art had relied on to build the company.

Dennis came in and hit the ground running. He was used to being the top dog. His most pressing mission was to knock me out of the number one spot in the company. He was running his version of the recruiting and building system and, for about six months, Dennis and I battled for that coveted number one spot.

I stayed focused on building a giant quality team committed to writing great quality business. My team had a deep and solid foundation that set us up to be earthquake-proof and to stand the test of time. Our relationships were our cement, and our training was our steel. Meanwhile, Dennis was taking short-cuts to hit his numbers. He wasn't following our success System properly, leaving out relationship building and sales training. Once that started coming to light, Dennis faded away. He never challenged me for the top spot again and was soon out of the company completely.

This was quite a testament to the power of our System. The stronger the foundation—inclusive of relationship building, earning trust, training, education, dream selling, and caring leadership—the higher and faster the building can rise, and the more stable it will be. Whether at a construction site or when building a business, the same principle applies.

CHAPTER 50

THE REAL HERO: NORMA HUMPHREY

I'VE MENTIONED IT BEFORE, BUT I CAN'T SAY ENOUGH ABOUT MY wife, Norma, and what a rock she was during this crazy time in our family's life. We moved away from her parents to live across the country. We were in a new city and in a house she hadn't picked out—one with a long, gross, dark-brown shag carpet she hated. Not only was she away from her folks, but she was away from her friends too, and she had four kids to get settled in scholastically and socially. On top of all of that, she was married to a man who was in serious pursuit of his dream to build a national business empire. A dream that demanded him to be on the road a tremendous amount of the time. I realized that no matter what, family came first, and with Norma's great help, we made sure that happened. I believe what she did during that time was more impressive than what I accomplished. I've said it a million times and I'll say it a million times more: There would be no Hubert without Norma.

Just like the System will save people from themselves, Norma has always saved me from myself. I like to think of it as her running the Family Format System. There's no telling where I would be without her. I believe in divine intervention and have no doubt God had a hand in putting me at the desk directly behind Norma in the third grade. We were close friends from the beginning, and over the next several years, we became teenage sweethearts as well. She has been the most influential person in my life ever since. Norma not only steered the family ship at home, she was the glue that held it together.

Our priorities have always been in this order: *God, family, business.* Every one of those three priorities is absolutely necessary all of the time, but there are certain moments and situations within each one where a particular *necessary* becomes *urgent,* and Norma was the one who made sure that, in the calendar of our life, the proper balance was always maintained.

Norma never let me get too full of myself, no matter how much of a big shot I thought I was. She stuck with me through my teasing her and always pulling her little blonde pigtails as she sat in the seat in front of me at school, through my rebellious teenage years, through us getting married and having children at a young age, through me leaving college early, and through the long hours I spent away for seventeen dangerous years on the railroad. She supported me in all of my church callings and responsibilities, never more than when I was asked, at age thirty, to be a bishop in our church, a lay ministry that required twenty to thirty hours a week of my time. She stood by my side through our tough financial times, miraculously handling our cash-strapped budget, enduring bill collectors, and always allowing me to pursue various business options, knowing how badly I wanted to leave the railroad. Norma kept me grounded through our rapid success and rise to fame, and she never stopped believing in me. She's never once ceased to be a rock for me and our four wonderful children: Jody, Kim, Jeffrey, and Jennifer.

Family and faith have always been most important to Norma and me. They have helped keep us grounded. With all the worldly successes that came our way, we had to do as Jesus Christ taught us, which, to paraphrase, was *to be in the world but not of the world.* With a life anchored in Jesus Christ, we did our best to build our family on that rock and not on the shifting sands of society. A great spiritual leader in our faith, David O. McKay, once declared: "No other success can compensate for failure in the home."[20] We built our family philosophy on that principle, and Norma was the driving force behind it.

Norma was my thermostat. She regulated me and thankfully didn't act like a thermometer, meaning she didn't just react to me. She kept me in line and made sure I didn't miss the most important things.

My plan was always to build up the West while based in Denver and then, within two or three years, move back to Georgia and continue the national expansion throughout the rest of the country. After our phenomenal life-changing success, we did indeed move back to Georgia in 1981. This time I had learned my lesson—Norma was going to approve where we moved to, and she was going to pick out our home too. We selected the growing city of Dunwoody. It is a beautiful suburb of Atlanta with gorgeous homes, excellent schools, a strong church community, and a perfect area to continue to build and raise a family. I am ever grateful to Norma for her tremendous influence and support throughout our life together.

CHAPTER 51

THE DOMINATION OF THE NATION— MOVING BACK TO GEORGIA!

So, AFTER LIVING IN DENVER FOR TWENTY-THREE MONTHS, WE moved to north Atlanta, near the company's new headquarters. I wanted to make sure that my influence was felt by Art and Boe, so I could give the most support to the Humphrey Worldwide Network team. My aim was also to spread our success and expand our team throughout the eastern US. Because I had built such a strong operation in Denver with wonderful leaders, I could move without worry.

I had taught by word and deed to so many of my leaders the principle of *repotting* oneself so more growth could happen. Now, once again, we uprooted, and this time we transplanted our family to Atlanta so we could continue our growth.

I had proven my System in Denver and in the Western states' expansion that followed. It worked even beyond my expectations. I went to Denver having been a railroad man making $27,000 a year, and only twenty-three months later I returned to Georgia as the number one guy in the fastest-growing company in the largest industry in the world (financial services), having recruited twenty-five thousand people to our team and making $1.4 million in 1981 (that's nearly $5.4 million in today's dollars). I had put my money where my mouth was, and I had delivered. I knew what I was doing. I now had a well-oiled machine. No one had any doubt now that our System could be successfully implemented by any leader in the company. I could look anyone in the eyes with confidence and tell them exactly what to do to succeed. I had moved to Denver knowing that Art had some misguided concerns about Amway. But, after the undeniable success of our System-building principles, I was well on my way to constructing what can best be described as *an Amway of insurance and mutual funds*. The company-wide success of my Leadership Format System concept gave Art's crusade the full distribution system that it needed.

Unlike most people who enjoy big success early on and become prematurely satisfied, mistaking the beginning for the end, my success had the opposite effect on me. It was like throwing gasoline on a fire. My vision was constantly being stretched. I was able to stay perpetually hungry and always driven to build bigger, faster, and higher.

Around this time, I was driving with my fifteen-year-old son, Jeff, when he asked me the same important question I'm often asked. He and his brother and sisters had been exposed to the business—they often helped around the office, we took them to meetings and on trips, and they had seen the leaders' bulletin. He asked why I was always at the top of the company while others came and went. He wanted to know how I was able to grow so fast and recruit so many people. My answer? I was fueled by a white-hot desire to succeed; I had a proven, simple, duplicatable System; and I never got bored with the basics.

You really need to watch as you achieve some success to be sure you don't get bored and forget what made you successful in the first place. NEVER GET TIRED OF DOING THE BASICS. Truth be told, I have done those same basics for over four decades in several companies. You may think I'm being dramatic by saying this, but if you go back and listen to talks I've given over the years, I doubt you'd be able to tell what year or what company it was. I found that the basics worked and there was never a need to change them. I'm sure most of you will recall the wonderful movie *Back to the Future*. I've always taught that by going "back in time" to the basics, you're ensuring your future. The landscape, technology, market conditions, and demographics may change, but the basics never do.

CHAPTER 52

WHAT YOU'RE LOOKING FOR IS LOOKING FOR YOU ... SO PURSUE IT: THE FRANCES AND LEE AVRETT STORY

BY NOW YOU KNOW THAT I WAS ON A QUEST TO FIND STRONG leaders who were driven, determined dreamers—leaders who were willing to learn, follow, and duplicate a successful System. Frances Avrett was such a leader.

I knew her from my Amway days. Frances and I were kindred spirits. We both loved the multiples and team-building aspects of Amway. When my family and I were about to move back to Georgia in 1981, I had a strong feeling that I should call her immediately to tell her about my tremendous success in Denver. Ironically, she had literally just left her house and was on her way to sign a contract with, of all things, another insurance company, where she would become what is referred to as a *captive agent.* Her family's financial situation at the time was such that she felt she had to finally surrender to this insurance agent who had been trying to recruit her for over a year. Just before she left to go and sign that contract, she ran back into the house to get her purse and heard the phone ringing! I caught her just in the nick of time. I told her not to sign anything until we talked.

When I arrived in Atlanta a week later, I drove down to rural Sandersville, Georgia, for an Opportunity Meeting with Frances and her husband, Lee. This first meeting was one to remember. It was held in the greenhouse nursery on their farm. Seven or eight of her prospects were there too. Before we even got started, the greenhouse sprinkler system went off and soaked all of us. When crazy stuff happens, you just have to roll with it. All I knew was that we had started a fire with this business that no sprinklers were going to put out.

Frances went on to build one of our greatest teams ever and also helped us pioneer ALW Canada. She did all of this while her husband was in poor health and while they were raising five children. She had a burning desire and a resolve to do whatever it took to succeed for her family's sake.

As you can see, it's important for you to act immediately when you feel these important promptings in your life. From that simple act of calling Frances when I did, thousands of lives have been positively changed forever.

CHAPTER 53

MOTIVATE THYSELF

I HAD BEEN NUMBER ONE IN THE COMPANY FOR SEVERAL YEARS, and everyone else was fighting for second place. Two of my chief competitors were Bob Turley and Ronnie Barnes, both of whom were ALW greats.

Bob was a former major league baseball player, a Cy Young Award–winning pitcher as well as a World Series champion for the New York Yankees. You may know him as "Bullet" Bob Turley. He was also one of the original seven Regional Vice Presidents at ALW.

Ronnie Barnes was a former high school teacher in Warner Robins, Georgia. He joined ALW around the same time I did. As he and his key leaders, including Kip Ridley, learned my Leadership Format System, he built one of the top teams in the company.

They were both pretty big leaders, but some of their growth came artificially, as Art placed various orphan teams under them. My team, by contrast, was not only much bigger, it had been built organically using our proven and duplicatable System. Our team took great pride in being the only *pure* Super Team at ALW.

I wanted to make a point to my hierarchy and the company that my System was the best way to build such a big hierarchy. I didn't want them to expect Art or me to give them ready-made teams. I'd seen an ad in a magazine showing the image of a man dressed as a professional salesperson on his left side and as an everyday person on his right side. With that in mind, I created a new image in my mind wherein one half was Ronnie and the other half was Bob. I named this new entity "Ronnie Turley" and began competing with both of their teams as if they were one big team. I liked both of them as people, but this helped to keep things exciting. I sent this image out to my team internally, and they loved it! Of course, Ronnie and Bob didn't love it so much because I continued to beat them month after month.

When the ALW company was formed, another one of Art Williams's original seven RVPs from his Waddell and Reed days became Art's chief team cheerleader of sorts, spending much of his career behind a desk at ALW headquarters. Right from the start, even though this individual was in a home office executive position, Art constantly put various team leaders in his downline under his overriding code number. Over the years, his prefabricated team's performance and production numbers provided the false perception that he was a great team builder. Of course, since I was holding myself out as having the only pure System-built hierarchy in the company, worthy of being copied by every agent hoping to build something great, I constantly reminded my team and my fellow competitors about his *favorite son* status just to keep the record straight.

Then one day, a few years later, I received a predictable call from another of Art's headquarter acolytes telling me that he had some good news for me. He said Art wanted to put one of the company's rising star's organizations under my hierarchy. I shocked him by politely telling him to let Art know that, while I appreciated his offer, I couldn't accept it, because the company needed at least one example of a great hierarchy that had been built from scratch using our System. I could tell this offer was the result of the chief team cheerleader's constant complaints

Leadership Legacy

WE HAVE A **GREAT FUTURE**

BECAUSE WE HAVE A **GREAT HISTORY**

BOXCAR TO BUSINESS STAR

I had an intense desire to make my dreams come true. Trapped in the midst of a grueling seventeen-year railroad career, I came to the realization that I could become anything I wanted to be. I worked hard and pursued many opportunities over the years until the right one finally came knocking at the door. The rest is business history.

THE FOUNDATION OF MY BUSINESS CAREER
SOUTHERN RAILWAY • 1962 - 1978
- Fueled desire to be my own boss
- Always searching for the right vehicle
- Instilled strong work ethic
- Never gave up on my dreams

AMWAY • 1968 - 1975
- First exposure to the networking industry
- Developed a recruiter's mentality
- Shaped a builder's mindset
- Learned the Secrets of Leadership
- Began to understand the magic of the multiples
- Became a student of human nature
- Learned the secrets of building large marketing teams
- Earned a promotion to direct distributor

BUSINESS CONDITIONS
- Dual crusade — "Everyone an entrepreneur" and "Replace lesser value products with greater value products"
- Simple story
- Viral
- No experience necessary
- No major investment required to get started
- Part-time/extra income
- Reposition old money to create
- Extra money to save
- Sold a dream

THE COMPANY
- I became one of the pioneers of network marketing
- Recruited millions of people through their system
- Business operations around the world

1954

1961

THE ENTREPRENEURIAL SPIRIT
My career began at age 12 with a succession of jobs to earn money, including grocery delivery boy, soda jerk, bakery employee, construction worker, and plumber's assistant.

School Days

1948-49

School Days

LOVE AT FIRST SIGHT
I met my future wife Norma Patrick in the third grade. We married in 1961. It has been true love ever since.

THE SEVENTEEN-YEAR J-O-B
In the summer of 1962 prior to my junior year in college, I took a job in Macon on the railroad. This "summer job" turned into a seventeen-year career as a conductor for southern railway, but I never shut down my dream machine. I was constantly searching for ways to escape my J-O-B.

THE FOUNDATION FOR A LEGACY

Our first home in Macon, Georgia was 1,145 sq. ft., but to both of us, it seemed huge.

My dream was financial independence for my family — Norma, Jody, Kim, Jeffrey, and Jennifer.

A BUILDER'S MINDSET IS BORN

In my search to be somebody, I tried many so-called "opportunities" with several different marketing companies. I spent seven years in the Amway business, learning the basics of recruiting and building large organizations. Who would have believed that I would later have tremendous success applying these powerful principles to the largest industries in the world?

As a new Amway direct distributor, I was preparing for the opportunity night meeting.

THE GREAT ESCAPE

When I joined A.L. Williams, I was more than prepared for the opportunity in front of me. In my first ninety days, I made more money part-time in ALW than I made full-time in an entire year on the railroad. It was obvious this was my chance for freedom.

The A.L. Williams office in Macon, where I was first exposed to the opportunity.

MVP OF THE NATIONAL CHAMPIONSHIP TEAM

From my humble part-time beginnings, I went on to build the largest and most successful team in A.L. Williams history. I produced and developed more than one thousand Regional Vice President and twenty five National Sales Directors worldwide. I broke every company record while leading ALW to seven straight national championships. I went on to win ALW's Leader of the Decade award, and my leadership legacy was born.

MY A.L. WILLIAMS TEAM TRACK RECORD
A.L. WILLIAMS • 1978 - 1991
- Earned $100,000 in commissions my first year
- First ALW leader to earn $ 1 million in 1 year
- First ALW leader to earn $2 million in 1 year
- First ALW leader to earn $3 million in 1 year
- Built the largest organization in ALW history
- Produced more $100,000 earners than any other organization
- 400,000 recruits/50,000 licensed associates
- Leaders in all 50 states, Canada, Puerto Rico, and Guam
- Named ALW's Leader of the Decade

BUSINESS CONDITIONS
- Crusade —"Buy Term and Invest the Difference"
- Simple story
- Viral
- No experience necessary
- No major investment required to get started
- Part-time/extra income
- Turmoil, high unemployment, and unrest in the market
- Reposition old money to create extra money to save
- $600 average commission per transaction
- Temporary license in early days of the company
- Sold a dream
- An idea whose time had come

THE COMPANY
- Leader of the "Buy Term and Invest the Difference" movement
- More than 1,000,000 people recruited
- The no.1 marketer of mutual funds
- The no.1 marketer of term insurance in the world— $350+ billion face amount
- Seven consecutive national championships
- Helped change the insurance buying habits of middle America

---

1978   **1979**

A TRUE CRUSADER

Fueled by my desire to want to be somebody and the "Buy Term and Invest the Difference" movement, I made over 135 personal sales in my first full year with ALW. I earned more than $100,000 and quickly became one of the ALW Heroes from All Walks of Life.

HOLD A MEETING

In July 1979, my family and I moved to Denver to lead ALW's Western expansion. More than 1,100 people joined my rapidly — growing organization in the first six months as I launched an unprecedented series of opportunity meetings throughout the west. The magic of compound recruiting was under way.

THE BIRTH OF THE SYSTEM

During my two years in Denver, more tha twenty five thousand people joined my business, and the Humphrey managemen factory system was born. This formatted system became the foundation for today's Leadership Format system.

HNN - A COMPANY WITHIN A COMPANY

In 1981, I moved my headquarters back to Atlanta and named my team the Humphrey National Network (HNN). Leaders from around the country would come to Atlanta to study my model and then return home to build their own empires.

THE RISE TO THE TOP

Hubert Humphrey Receives Double Honors

I was promoted by Art Williams to the exclusive NSD position and named to the Board of Directors due to my record-breaking success in the field.

ALW LEADER OF THE DECADE

As a result of my hard work, which produced more $100,000 earners and more senior leadership than any other organization in the company, I was named ALW's Most Valuable Leader of the Decade in 1987.

A.L. WILLIAMS NATIONAL CHAMPIONS

I was first through the banner at a company convention at Boca Raton in December 1984 to celebrate the company's victory over Prudential and the rest of the industry in total face amount of life insurance written. A one hundred fifty-year dynasty had been defeated.

INSPIRING A NEW GENERATION OF BUILDERS

Art Williams personally commissioned me to write a book on the secrets of building a super hierarchy. *The Magic of Compound Recruiting* inspired thousands of leaders to make their dreams come true by running a system whereby recruiting never stops.

HWN - TAKING THE OPPORTUNITY WORLDWIDE

With expansion into Canada and Puerto Rico, I renamed my organization the Humphrey Worldwide Network. I started traveling in my own private jet to visit my rapidly growing global team of more than twenty five thousand leaders.

A LEADERSHIP TEAM FOR THE AGES

This is a snapshot of my leadership team at its peak in the ALW era. It was the prototype for the perfectly running model and the ultimate example of building with geometric progression- wide and deep.

WORLD MARKETING ALLIANCE (WMA) TEN YEARS OF BUSINESS GREATNESS

In 1991, I left my former company to pursue my bold new vision to create a different kind of company, designed to attract entrepreneurs from all walks of life to come and do their best work. From day one, WMA was committed to leading the investment revolution and helping build financial security for families worldwide. The movement helped thousands of WMA families achieve record-breaking business success. This courageous leadership team set in motion an extraordinary series of accomplishments that continue to shape the destiny of millions.

WMA LEADERSHIP & TRACK RECORD
WMA • 1991 - 2001
- 1,500+ $100,000 earners
- 2,500+ $50,000 earners
- 50,000+ insurance - licensed associates
- 12,000+ securities - licensed associates
- 8,000+ mortgage associates
- 500+ p & c - licensed associates

BUSINESS CONDITIONS
- Crusade —"Variable Universal Life (VUL) to middle America" (tax advantages of life insurance & investment advantages of mutual funds)
- An idea whose time had come
- Consumers eager to learn how money works
- Bull market
- No clear competition
- Right place at the right time
- High barriers to entry
- Required new money
- Highly regulated industry - complex products
- $1,800 average commission per transaction
- Uncertainty in stock market conditions created doubts and fears about investing
- In the end, the industry changed and the window started to close.

THE COMPANY
- Leader of the variable product movement
- Taking Wall Street to Main Street
- More than 400,000 people recruited
- More than one billion dollars in commissions paid to the field
- Total sales of over four billion dollars
- One of the largest independent marketers of financial services products
- Helped change the investment habits of middle America

THE ODYSSE BEGINS
The original founders of WM made the infamous bus trip t Western Reserv Life to kickoff t new era.

I ANNOUNCED "ALEXANDER, INC." TO THE WORLD IN THE USA TODAY.
The company would soon change to World Marketing Alliance, Inc. to better reflect WMA's global vision of leading the investment revolution.

A SYSTEM WHEREBY RECRUITING NEVER STOPS

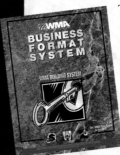

The Business Format Syste stood as a blueprint to help all WMA associates build and run successful businesses. It represented the next step in the evolution of the my Humphrey managemen factory system.

With operations rapidl expanding across the globe, we relocated to WMA's new headquarte building in 1995.

FROM GREAT EVENT TO GREAT EVENT

World-class events were the lifeblood for creating momentum in WMA. From the first company convention in Las Vegas in 1992 attended by two thousand hopeful associates to the giant world conventions attended by more than twenty thousand, the company's history was set against a back-drop of big events. These meetings represented the best the company had to offer — from outstanding field leaders to some of the world's most dynamic guest speakers from the business, sports, and entertainment world to the most spectacular recognition ceremonies in business history — to inspire a new generation of leaders.

General H. Norman Schwarzkopf

Bestselling Author Stephen R. Covey

Astronaut Buzz Aldrin, one of the first men to walk on the moon

"The Greatest" Muhammad Ali

Super Bowl III MVP and Hall of Fame quarterback Joe Namath

Legendary World Champion Coach Pat Riley

The world's foremost peak performance coach Tony Robbins

Tom Peters, the bestselling business author of all time

Renowned financial prognosticator Harry Dent and I in Hawaii

Me and Huey Lewis & The News

The Beach Boys' Mike Love

The Pointer Sisters

CONQUEST OF PARADISE...THE ANNUAL HAWAII TRIP

More than any other destination, Hawaii came to symbolize WMA's "home-away-from-home" reward for top leaders. We spared no expense while taking thousands of winning couples to the most luxurious resorts throughout the Hawaiian Islands. This annual trip to paradise became one of WMA's greatest traditions.

1991–2001 | 1995 | 1998

WORLD CLASS SUPPORT NETWORK

WMA built a world class support network of companies that uniquely positioned us to meet the financial challenges of consumers.

WMA SECURITIES, INC.   WMA MORTGAGE SERVICES, INC.

WMA INVESTMENT ADVISORS, INC.   THE WMA CORPORATION

MD TV

MD TV, the company's private satellite television network, served as a dynamic medium to get instant business-building ideas and motivation to WMA leaders around the world.

WMA GOES GLOBAL

WMA expanded its powerful business operations to Canada, Taiwan, Mexico, Puerto Rico, Guam, and the Philippines, taking the opportunity worldwide.

PREFERRED PRODUCT PROVIDERS

WMA represented some of the largest and most powerful companies in the financial services industry, including Western Reserve Life, American Skandia, Zurich Kemper, Pacific Life, Fortis, The Midland, and many more. This network gave WMA a diversified product portfolio to meet the needs of families around the world.

WMA RECEIVED NATIONA

WMA EXECUTIVE WORL

March 23, 1998 marked the historic dedication for the new WMA executive world headquarters, which served as dream central for our expansion worldwide. This state-of-the-ar 100,000 square foot building housed WMA's more than five hundred employees to support our rapidly-growing field team.

OUR GREAT SUPER TRI

Paris, Rome, Monte Carlo, London, Venice, Munich, Salzburg, Vienna, and Floren all served as the backdrop for the grand Search for Alexander tradition. Winners received the royal treatment at the most exclusive resorts throughout Europe.

WORLD CLASS RECOGNITIO

WMA recognized its greatest leaders with everything from custom super bowl-type rings to Rolex watches to custom wall of fame portraits to majestic swords to alexanders, our own exclusive version of the Oscar.

EDIA ATTENTION

Featured on MSNBC

WMA CEO Hubert Humphrey and
WMA President Wood Montgomery

EADQUARTERS

RADITION...THE SEARCH FOR ALEXANDER

REWARD

WORLD LEADERSHIP GROUP... A COMPANY OF DESTINY

In 2001, my grand vision soared to an entire new level. Having sold WMA to The AEGON Group, my leadership team and I were then ready to build our greatest company ever. A whole new world of opportunity was suddenly on the horizon. World Leadership Group offered an exciting new business opportunity based on revolutionary new strategies combined with the proven business systems from our past successes. Leadership, Experience, Track Record ...World Leadership Group stood as one of our historic, legendary success companies.

THE GRAND VISION OF WLG
WORLD LEADERSHIP GROUP
- Our Vision – led the consumer empowerment revolution
- Our Mission – created more financially independent families than any other business in history
- Our System – the vehicle that allowed us to achieve our Vision and our Mission

BUSINESS CONDITIONS
- Two Crusades –
- "Harness the power of your mortgage to build wealth" and
- "Harness the For Sale By Owner real estate concept to build wealth"
- Simple story
- Viral
- No experience required
- No major investment required to get started
- Part-time/extra Money
- We sell a Dream
- Turmoil, high unemployment, and unrest in the market
- Reposition old money to create extra money to save
- $3,200 average commission per mortgage transaction
- Instant start-up – no license required in most states
- An idea whose time has come

(Continued)

HOW TO WIN THE MONEY GAM

World Lending Group was one of the nation's premier mortgage lenders/ brokers that offered a diversified portfol of revolutionary concepts and products from more than one hundred of the mos respected companies in the industry.

WHAT THE EXPERTS SAID...

"Carrying a mortgage doesn't cause you to lose any money at all. In fact, just the opposite is true: carrying a mortgage is actually quite profitable. It's eliminating the mortgage that forces you to give up profitable opportunities.

"If you have a mortgage and you're dreaming of the day when you make your final payment, you're trying to do something that financially successful people do not do."
— Ric Edelman, *New York Times* bestselling author of *Ordinary People, Extraordinary Wealth*

World Realty Group offered marketing services to the "For Sale by Owner" customer as well as discounted real estate commissions from our network of full-service brokers® to create a "no-risk solution" for homeowners.

WE SUCCESSFULLY HELPED TO CHANGE AMERICA'S MORTGAGE AND REAL ESTATE BUYING HABITS.

SCENARIO NO. 1

$200,000 MORTGAGE

**TRADITIONAL
30-YEAR LOAN**

$1,297
Mortgage payment

**ADJUSTABLE
RATE LOAN**

$1,119
Mortgage payment

CHOOSE ONE OF THE ABOVE

SCENARIO NO. 2

$200,000 MORTGAGE

**TRADITIONAL LOAN
(30-YEAR FIXED RATE)**

$1,297
Mortgage payment

**POWER OPTION LOAN
(OPTION ARM)**

$838
Mortgage payment

CHOOSE ONE OF THE ABOVE

The power option lets you choose your payment each and every month

OPTION ONE: |$838 MONTH

Payment based on an introductory start rate for the first 12 months.

OPTION TWO: |$1,039 MONTH

Interest-only payment set up on a so-year schedule.

OPTION THREE: |$1,229 MONTH

Payment based on a fully-amortized 30-year loan.

OPTION FOUR: |$1,713 MONTHS

Payment based on a fully-amortized 15-year loan.

$200,000 MORTGAGE

**TRADITIONAL REAL
ESTATE SALE**

$12–14,000
Real estate commissions

**FOR SALE BY OWNER
REAL ESTATE SALE**

$1,595
Marketing fee

CHOOSE ONE OF THE ABOVE

WRG'S FSBO PACKAGE INCLUDES:

EDUCATION
WRG provides all of the knowledge and tips needed to sell your own home.

EXPOSURE
Our web site, distinctive yard sign, 24-hour information hotline, and call center ensure maximum exposure to the marketplace.

RESOURCES
Strategic alliances with vendors to give our sellers a competitive advantage

A "NO RISK" SOLUTION
One of the greatest benefits of the WRG real estate concept is the plan allows you to list the home at any time with a WRG affiliated network Realtor for a commission of only 4%.

THE COMPANIES

World Leadership Group
- An independent marketing company offered people from all walks of life the opportunity to be in business for themselves, but not by themselves, while helping families get better value for their money.

World Lending Group
- One of the nation's premier lender/brokers offered a diversified portfolio of mortgage concepts and products.

World Realty Group
- Offered marketing solutions to "For Sale By Owner" customers to help them save substantial money when selling their home

REVOLUTIONARY COMPENSATION

WLG allowed people from all walks of life the opportunity to build a business with:

- Programs that allow you to get off to a fast start without expensive and time consuming licensing processes.
- Complete field training program that allows you to "earn while you learn."
- Great personal production contracts from 30-90%.
- Incredible Infinity Builders Plan with revenue spreads as high as 60% on new associates you bring into your business.
- Plus six generations of overrides on your RMDs and up.

Norma and I travel the world to build the business in our luxurious Gulfstream jet.

GREAT PART-TIME OPPORTUNITY

You get started today building your business and become a Senior Associate:

Close 1 loan a month... $2,000/mo.
Close 1 WRG package a month... $350/mo.
Close 4 loans a month... $8,000/mo.*
Close 4 WRG Packages a month... $1,400/mo.

What would this type of part-time income mean to you?

Close 1 loan a month and save the money for retirement
over 30 years ...
@ 4% = $1,624,517
@ 8% = $4,520,976

WHERE ELSE CAN YOU MAKE THIS KIND OF MONEY PART-TIME?

INFINITY BUILDERS PLAN

You become an RMD Leader and build a Team:

Close 4 loans a month
personally... $10,240/mo.

You build 5 Associates who each close 2 loans a month... $13,600/mo.

You become an NMD and build 6 direct RMD Leaders:

Base Shop
Income... $30,560/mo.

6 direct RMD Leaders producing the same volume
— 4 loans a month personally with a team of 5 associates each closing 2 loans a month... $36,000/mo.

Let's assume each of those RMD Leaders become AMDs and build 3 RMD Leaders each:

Base Shop
Income... $30,560/mo.

6 direct AMD Leaders with 3 RMD Leaders each producing the same volume
— 4 loans a month personally with a team of 5 associates each closing 2 loans a month ... $98,400/mo.

Base Shop Income:	$23,840/mo.	Total Income:	$66,560/mo.	Total Income:	$128,960/mo.

HEGEMON GROUP INTERNATIONAL
AN INTEGRITY][COMPANY

A NEW ERA BEGINS WITH HGI

In 2014, I founded HGI, which recruits and trains advisors who serve the life insurance needs of thousands of families and continues to grow at a record-breaking pace. HGI has expanded to include nearly, ten thousand licensed agents across the U.S. and Canada.

With HGI's impressive growth, HGI Associates will secure more than $200 million in annual life insurance premiums and over $400 million in annual annuity premiums. Over the last three years, these HGI Associates have secured more than $40 billion in face amount for the clients they serve.

Each year, our company hosts several premier training events designed to inspire, educate, and recognize our incredibly driven field agents. The year kicked off with TOP GUN, an electrifying event in January that set the stage for success. In the spring, top performers earned a spot in CONQUEST OF PARADISE, an exclusive, qualifier-only trip to the breathtaking islands of Hawaii, blending luxury with learning.

Later in the year, RMD ACADEMY offered an intensive training experience focused on leadership and business development. Finally, the summer brought the CONVENTION OF CHAMPIONS, our flagship event that celebrates achievement, growth, and the power of our collective success. These events are key to fostering motivation, growth, and excellence within our organization.

"IT TAKES LEADERS WITH VISION TO HELP PEOPLE WITH DREAMS. WE'VE ALWAYS BEEN IN THE BUSINESS OF MAKING DREAMS COME TRUE WORLDWIDE."

HGI Founder &
CEO Hubert Humphrey

A NEW GENERATION OF LEADERS

We are building a new generation of leaders who are learning from the legends of the past and driving progress faster, bigger, and better than ever before. Akki and Ronak Roopani, one of the most powerful couples in financial services history, are prime examples of this philosophy in action. In just six short years, they've become the flagship leadership team at HGI, following in the footsteps of the great iconic leaders that I developed in his previous ALW and WMA Ventures. Their expertise in my team building, product, and financial education has set new standards. He is projected to hit the $10 million annual earnings level soon. Thanks to the power of the Leadership Format System, HGI has produced several more million dollar earners and Super Team builders.

HEGEMON GROUP INTERNATIONAL

AN INTEGRITY][COMPANY

2022

INTEGRITY MARKETING GROUP

HGI partnered with integrity on May 25, 2022, to innovate insurance and serve more Americans.

I selected Integrity for its best-in-class technology in marketing support capabilities to provide more comprehensive solutions to our advisors and clients.

HGI is an independent marketing company that is bringing Wall Street to Main Street. No matter what financial challenges clients may face, HGI has the experience and resources to create a successful financial plan. HGI's experienced associates have taught clients about the "Circle of Safety." In these unprecedented financial times, it is important to help clients preserve their capital, while seeking long term growth and appreciation. HGI's associates are among the most educated and well-trained in the industry.

HGI Founder & CEO Hubert Humphrey
With Integrity Marketing
CEO Bryan W. Adams

Akki Roopani, EVC was the top recipient among many other great leaders to participate in the HGI Equity Share Program.

"I'M ALWAYS LOOKING FOR THE NEXT MODERN DAY ALEXANDERS, PEOPLE LIKE MYSELF WHO HAVE THAT BURNING DESIRE TO MAKE THEIR DREAMS COME TRUE. MY GREATEST REWARDS IN MY BUSINESS LIFE HAVE BEEN FROM HELPING OTHER PEOPLE ACHIEVE TREMENDOUS SUCCESS."

HGI Founder & CEO
Hubert Humphrey

WORLD-CLASS TRIPS

In the summer of 2023, I took top leaders and corporate executives on an unforgettable journey through Europe on Search for Alexander. This exclusive trip, named after my icon-Alexander the Great-was not just an adventure but also a powerful leadership experience. We explored Paris, Florence, and Rome, immersing ourselves in some of the world's most historic landmarks. From walking through the Roman colosseum and visiting Napoleon's tomb to enjoying a breathtaking dinner at the Eiffel tower and discovering ancient ruins, every moment reflected the timeless qualities of leadership and vision. As we savored world-famous cuisine and connected with one another, we were reminded of Alexander's remarkable ability to inspire and lead. The Search for Alexander was a true celebration of leadership, legacy, and success, aligning perfectly with our company's commitment to nurturing leaders who leave a lasting impact.

A FINANCIAL INDUSTRY POWERHOUSE

Hegemon Group International is rapidly establishing itself as a powerhouse in the financial industry, experiencing unprecedented growth and dominance. With over fifty thousand agents across the nation, HGI has already served more than one hundred thousand families, providing them with unparalleled financial solutions that help secure their futures. HGI has paid out nearly $500 million in commissions, a clear indicator of the massive success and opportunity available to both agents and clients alike. The company's growth is further fueled by its strategic partnerships with top-tier product providers, ensuring agents have access to the best financial products on the market. Backed by Integrity Marketing Group, one of the most respected names in the industry. HGI's dominance is not only driven by innovation but also by a commitment to integrity and excellence. As the company continues to scale, it remains on track to reshape the financial landscape, setting new standards for success and industry leadership. This is only just the beginning for our future.

ELITE SUPER TEAM BUILDERS THA

Akki Roopani

...WILL LEAD HGI INTO THE FUTURE.

Raghu Reddy

Prashant Morajkar

Altaf Hemdani

Jody Humphrey

Following the Leadership Format System turns you in to Superman. This is me on the left in July of 1983 at our convention in Boca Raton, Florida and on the right is me forty years to the month at our convention in Vegas.

Norma is the most wonderful friend, wife, and business partner a person can ever have.
She has influenced my life more than any person I've ever known.

to Art that I wasn't playing fair. You can imagine the shock that my refusal caused.

This insult to the integrity of my team-building System mindset motivated me to become even more competitive. I decided to declare war on this great pretender, the cheerleader in chief. I wrote a letter to the Humphrey Worldwide Network (HWN) and to all the builders of ALW. It was time, once and for all, for our team to blow these fabricated teams away. In my best imitation of President Franklin D. Roosevelt's Pearl Harbor speech to Congress, I sent something that began like this: "Today, a day that will live in infamy, Hubert Humphrey and the HWN have declared business competitive warfare, in particular, on the cheerleader's fabricated hierarchy!" Needless to say, it had the intended effect. I must admit here that all of this was done in the spirit of good-natured competition.

All of my self-motivation psychologies kept me energized, driven, and razor-sharp. Competition is a great thing—it keeps everybody awake. I know this made the company a lot of money, as everyone brought their A-game to try to best me. We were all friends who competed like hell against each other. Today, I look back on them as great friends who not only contributed to my success but also contributed to the success of the whole ALW company and legacy. As I subsequently became founder and CEO of several great companies, I constantly reflected on those experiences and saw the reasoning behind many of Art's decisions.

I'm reminded of a simple little cassette tape brought to me by a recruit a few years earlier in our Denver days. I was intrigued by the title, "Who Motivates the Motivator?" After listening to it one night, I found out the surprising answer— "The Motivator does!"

You've got to motivate yourself!!!

CHAPTER 54

OUR WAR CRY: BEAT PRUDENTIAL!

ALW WAS A DISRUPTING FORCE IN THE LIFE INSURANCE INDUSTRY. What had started out as just a little marketing group with a ragtag, part-time army quickly became a dominant industry player. Art never forgave the insurance industry for how they took so much money and provided so little value to those who needed it most. So, from the very beginning, he set out to build a business that would beat Prudential and take on the industry as a whole.

As you know by now, when I met Art Williams he burned with a crusade-like passion. All he lacked was a great distribution system. I was directly and indirectly responsible for more than 80 percent of the company's business, in large part due to the power of the distribution team-building System I brought with me.

In December 1983, while we were at a big ALW conference held at a resort in Boca Raton, Florida, Boe Adams invited me to breakfast to go over a strategic idea he had. Knowing the intensity and value of the building and travel schedule I had maintained—on average, I was spending more than 250 nights away from home for the previous four years—he knew he had to do something to protect the company's major asset. So, he proposed that he and I be fifty-fifty partners in the purchase of a jet, and I agreed. I ended up using it 95 percent of the time, but he didn't mind because he knew that it was going to be a force multiplier for the company, as it would lessen a lot of travel wear and tear on me and allow me more time with my family. Boe's strategic mentorship was the catalyst for my extraordinary business longevity. This turned out to be one of the great game changers in my career; it led to me having thirteen more jets over the next forty years, which my leaders and I used to build our great teams.

Armed with my Leadership Format System and Art's crusade to replace expensive cash value life insurance policies with inexpensive, high-coverage term insurance, ALW declared business warfare on Prudential, the perennial national champions of the insurance industry.

In 1984, six short years after we started, ALW outsold the largest insurance company in the world, 109-year-old industry giant Prudential, by writing $66 billion of face amount to their $53 billion. As the small "David" in the giant financial services arena, we had stared down and conquered one of the largest companies in the biggest industry in the world! And like David, who had faith in his simple but powerful sling to slay the giant Goliath and save his nation, ALW helped save Middle America.

At first Prudential probably didn't know we were gunning for them, and if they did, I'm sure they weren't too scared. Goliath never gave a second thought to the diminutive David calling him out from the other side. But our faith was unshakable. After beating Prudential, the perpetual number one player in the industry, Art declared us the new national champions of insurance in 1984. We were no longer the hunters; we were now the hunted.

As effective as Art was in building the great ALW company, I would have loved to see him realize his first dream of becoming a great college football coach. I'm confident he would have succeeded at the level of his hero, Paul "Bear" Bryant, the legendary head coach of the University of Alabama's football team. Art, in his role as a coach for ALW, is probably most famous for his "Do-It" speech—the talk he'd give to get everyone primed for success. When most of our team members would eventually ask him what the *it* was in that command, he always answered, "Whatever it takes!"

As we took on the largest industry in the world (the first one to measure its sales in the trillions), we exposed them for what they really were. As stated in Andrew Tobias's great book *The Invisible Bankers*, they were "the world's largest banking entity selling these cash value whole life policies to gather enormous assets."[21] He also described how the assets in all the banks in the country paled in comparison to the cash value assets in the coffers of the cash value life insurance companies. We indeed became the Robin Hood of the industry that we had set out to be—taking from the rich insurance companies and giving back to Middle America.

CHAPTER 55

THE MAGIC OF COMPOUND RECRUITING

IN 1984, I DECIDED TO PUBLISH A BOOK, *THE MAGIC OF Compound Recruiting*, explaining my recruiting and building System for the entire company. I detailed the philosophy and mindset that went along with the System that had been so effective. The book took off, spreading not only across ALW, but throughout the larger financial services industry, and then beyond to other network marketing organizations. The success of ALW demonstrated that if a recruiting and building distribution model worked in the complicated and highly regulated financial services industry, it could be viable in many other industries as well.

The Magic of Compound Recruiting outlined steps that, if followed, could lead to the great success that I, and many of my leaders, had achieved. I laid it all out, not keeping any success secrets from anyone who wanted to learn them. The approach was simple: Run the System as outlined, do it repeatedly, teach others to do it, and never get tired of the basics.

Compound Recruiting is the key. Just like the difference between simple interest and compound interest you receive from a bank, there is a powerful difference between *Simple Recruiting* and Compound Recruiting. For example, if you invested $1,000 at 3 percent simple interest, you would receive $30 once. However, if you earned 3 percent compound interest on that same $1,000 principle, you not only would make the $30 at

3 percent simple interest, but this $30 of interest reinvested would earn interest, and that interest would also earn interest, and so on. Likewise, if you only develop a single Simple Recruit, you only get the result of what that recruit can produce. But if you use our System's Taprooting and Overlapping Leadership principles, that single recruit will possibly develop recruits who will develop recruits exponentially, with all of the production that comes with those new team members.

System Recruiting leads to Compound Recruiting, Compound Production, and Compound Cash Flow. By applying the Magic of Compound Recruiting, you have a system whereby recruiting never stops, warm leads never stop, production never stops, promotions never stop, cash flow never stops, and training never stops.

But also—leaders never cease rising to the top.

CHAPTER 56

MY SECOND EPIPHANY:
I HAVE "THE ALEXANDER COMPLEX"

By 1989, I had achieved tremendous success. I had overcome many obstacles, escaped a dangerous seventeen-year career on the railroad, and become an American rags-to-riches story. I owned a beautiful mansion, had purchased several private jets, and had significant wealth. I was number one in the fastest-growing company in the entire financial services industry. We were holding massive meetings and conventions and had our Hero-Making machine cranking.

During this time, I would often be asked what kept me going. What caused me to keep expanding my vision? Why didn't I just coast and rest on my success? The simple answer is I feared that if I stopped, someone else would pass me by. I would never dare to even think about coasting.

I was always reading books about great military, political, spiritual, and business leaders. I hoped that their stories might help me see what I needed to do to make my dreams come true. All the while, I kept my Trying Motor running. As my dreams got bigger, so did my successes. I was a man in a hurry, always in search of the next great world to conquer.

One day, Frances Avrett and I were flying in my private jet to Los Angeles for a meeting. During the flight, I had an epiphany that would change the course of financial services history. I had received a preview of Michael Meyer's book *The Alexander Complex*. I read on the jacket cover how six great businessmen—Steve Jobs,

Ross Perot, James Rouse, Robert Swanson, Ted Turner, and Daniel Ludwig—all had something he called "The Alexander Complex."

I didn't know much about Alexander at the time, except that he was a Greek leader who had conquered the known world. I'm sure thankful I followed Alexander the Great, because I still don't know what happened to that fellow Alexander the Average and Ordinary.

I learned what the author meant by the Alexander Complex, which was that each of these businessmen had *noble ideas* and wanted to conquer the business world for *noble purposes*. This mirrored what Alexander the Great had done when he set out to conquer the world by conquering the hearts of men and introducing the noble Greek way of life as he went. According to the book, this made Alexander different from his father, King Philip II of Macedonia, who conquered lands but couldn't rule. At the core of Alexander's dream was a "divine restlessness"—a belief in the inevitability of his vision, instilled in him as a young boy by Aristotle while studying at his academy. Alexander was in the "grip of his vision"—a vision he could no more let go of than he could stop breathing. This book, *The Alexander Complex*, revealed the secret.

As I read the following passage, it took my breath away and made me sit ramrod straight with my mouth wide open:

> Alexander's feats defy the skeptics. You can better appreciate the sweep of the man by imagining him in business, arguably the last frontier in today's more circumscribed world. Corporate raiders would be sardines to Alexander's shark. **His sprawling holding company, Alexander, Inc.** would span a dozen advancing technologies, from supercomputers to bioengineering. Alexander's philanthropic

works might serve as a standard of public-spiritedness for decades, perhaps even generations. So would his reputation for toughness. He inspired men to follow him to the ends of the earth...[22]

This stunned me to the point where I exclaimed, "That's it!" so loudly it startled Frances. I read the words repeatedly as the idea took on a life of its own. *Alexander, Inc.* The very thought of it captured my imagination and stirred my soul.

"Frances, I just saw our future!" I said to her excitedly. "I know where we're going now." I had been supercharged!

Everything I had been doing—the big ideas, the growth, selling dreams, building leaders—it was all leading up to this epiphany. Right there, reading *The Alexander Complex* on that flight, I finally had a name for everything I had been building and everything I would ever build going forward: *Alexander Inc., The Big Idea.*

I even called my wife that night, excitedly telling her that I'd finally found the answer to her question, "What is causing you to be so driven?" I told her that I now realized I had The Alexander Complex!

Like Alexander, I was also in the "grip of a vision." And once my mind expanded to something that big, it flowed into everything else. I supersized the rest of my business life. I had an even bigger purpose now. I built bigger teams, held bigger meetings, bought bigger jets and bigger mansions. My hunger and drive became insatiable and unstoppable. But most importantly, *I was able to inspire all of my leaders to catch this very same vision, which would change their lives forever.* They saw that I was caught up in this great new way of seeing things, and they excitedly shared it with me. They had been following the *average-sized* Hubert

Humphrey, but now they were following the *supersized* Hubert Humphrey! Since that flight, I have been building upon the concept of *Alexander Inc., The Big Idea,* day in and day out, every single day. I became a *vision stretcher* and a *paradigm shifter* for all of our people, helping them dream bigger and achieve more than they ever could have before.

All of this happened because I lived the various principles I've outlined in this book. As a result, I was ready to take my team, Humphrey Worldwide Network, that I had built within ALW, and rename it: Alexander, Inc.

Alexander the Great sold his dream to others, aimed at their hearts, and convinced them to align with something bigger than themselves. These are the very same principles that I have always taught our leaders.

Since Alexander is not alive to complete what Michael Meyer described as "Alexander, Inc.," I took it upon myself to become a Modern-Day Alexander and to develop an ever-growing army of Alexander-like Business Warriors and Warrior Generals who could build this idea of a Modern-Day Alexander, Inc., and conquer the financial services business world with me.

CHAPTER 57

CONSTANCY AMID CHANGE

A PRINCIPLE THAT'S BEEN FOUNDATIONAL TO MY SUCCESS IS called *Constancy Amid Change*. It means that while many things in the world have changed over my several decades in business, there have always been constant principles woven throughout each phase of my career that don't change.

I first learned of the Constancy Amid Change concept in 1979 from the teachings of one of the apostles in my church, N. Eldon Tanner. While technology, economic conditions, demographics, and many other worldly things are changing, certain core principles never change. Just as there are constant principles that apply to success in life, there are constant principles that apply to success in business, including working hard, working smart, running a system, exhibiting leadership and followership, and making people's dreams come true. These are just a few of the important things that remain unchanged. My core vision of what I wanted to be and how I wanted to build my business has been constant throughout my career. Having a foolproof, profitable, and duplicatable system for people to follow is the mechanism for making it happen.

There's never been a device invented that can look into the heart of a person to determine whether or not they'll be successful. People can't see the desires of your heart, either, so don't let the doubters tell you that you can't succeed. Whether you choose to pursue success with us, or adopt these principles in your own individual endeavor, it is my hope that they will help you have the success you seek.

Are *you* a candidate who wants to participate in something as big as Alexander, Inc.?

CHAPTER 58

BE A DO-IT-FIRST LEADER

I WAS DRIVEN TO CONSTANTLY BUILD MY PERSONAL MASTER-COPY prototype Base Shop so it would inspire my downline leaders to constantly build their Base Shop. This meant that I stayed in the trenches, on the front line, and continuously, personally recruited new, Driven, Determined Dreamers into my Base Shop. This is what I mean when I say be a *Do-It-First Leader.*

On the day we moved back to Georgia, we were chatting with one of our new neighbors, when he asked me what I did for work and the conversation somehow turned to income. I told him I made about $50,000–$60,000. He thought I was talking annually, but when I explained that I made that monthly, he perked up. Needless to say, being the savvy businessman that he was, he became my first recruit in my new Atlanta Base Shop and one of my first-generation RVP promotions.

Having a strong Base Shop was a point of pride for me. More importantly, it kept me in the game, ensuring that I remained sharp and engaged, giving me the moral authority to be a strong leader worthy of being duplicated. I loved personal recruiting, i.e., bringing in new blood and helping change people's lives. Many leaders get out of the trenches and start leading from the back once they have a little success under their belt. But not me. I have studied and love so many of the great military leaders of the Heroic Era of war—such as Alexander the Great—who had such a strong do-as-I-do mentality that men literally followed them into battle.

Since the invention of the gun and bullets, we have been living in the Post-Heroic Era. Leaders now lead from the back, waging war from a computer screen in the safety of a room far removed from the battle. From a business standpoint, that is not how to show leadership. There is no faster way to lose credibility than to ask your team to do something that you're not willing to do. The reason people have always followed me is that *I've never asked them to do something I wasn't currently doing. The first principle of leadership is followership.* I was always willing to follow and submit to a proven System of success.

CHAPTER 59

LEADERS WITH VISION HELPING PEOPLE WITH DREAMS

AN EFFECTIVE LEADER MUST HAVE A CLEAR VISION TO KEEP THEIR team focused. Two scriptures in the Bible illustrate the importance of leading with vision much better than I ever could:

"Where there is no vision, the people perish" (Proverbs 29:18).

"And if the blind lead the blind, both shall fall into the ditch" (Matthew 15:14).

I have learned that clarity of vision will help you survive the ups and downs of being your own boss. When you wake up in the morning with a clear vision of your future, that day becomes effective and efficient.

You can't necessarily stretch your own vision, but you can make the conscious decision to expose yourself to events, people, and circumstances that can help stretch your vision. The same goes for your team. As a Director of Motivation, you must direct your team to events where their vision can be extended. In most cases, for your vision to be stretched in a meaningful way, you must go through a deep emotional experience. This is how Walt Disney built his team of Imagineers to help keep his company's dream machine always creating new successes.

It's hard to achieve success if you've never seen it or envisioned it. Look at the "Six Steps to Turn Your Desires into Gold" in *Think and Grow Rich* and you'll see why envisioning your success is so important:

"Step 1—Determine in your mind the exact amount of money you desire."

It is not sufficient merely to say, "I want plenty of money." Be definite as to the amount. (And think BIG! "I want to generate $1 million a year in revenues.")

"Step 2—Determine exactly what you intend to give in return for the money you desire."

Your goal should be to help others solve a problem or provide something of value. It's hard to amass a fortune by not doing either one or both of these.

"Step 3—Establish a definite date when you intend to possess the money you desire." I like to set a date three years out.

"Step 4—Create a definite plan for carrying out your desire, and begin at once, whether you are ready or not, to put this plan into action.

"Step 5—Write out a clear, concise statement of the amount of money you intend to acquire, name the time limit for its acquisition, state what you intend to give in return for the money, and describe clearly the plan through which you intend to accumulate it.

"Step 6—Read your written statement aloud, twice daily, once just before retiring at night, and once after arising in the morning. As you read—SEE and FEEL and BELIEVE yourself already in possession of the money."[23]

Having vision is not just about the head and eyes. The vision I'm talking about has to be felt. This is why I teach people to recruit by *aiming for the heart and trusting that the head will follow*. Thoughts in the brain are just data or *head thinking*, but, once they go to the heart and become *heart thinking*—once they get emotionalized, the vision and feelings naturally become stretched.

It wasn't good enough for me to have a vision and then make that vision a reality. I kept dreaming and having my vision expanded again and again. With each expansion, my successes became bigger and bigger, and so did my team's success. I felt that if I didn't have a new vision, my success would stall and eventually perish. My dream machine got stuck in the on position. I would stand on the shoulders of the old me and have my vision expanded in order to become the new me. As I was going through this perpetual vision-stretching, patience was key. Boe Adams shared this wisdom with me: "Hubert, you need to give yourself enough time for your efforts to compound." Massive growth doesn't happen overnight, but I was doing the right things, so with patience, the growth would come. This was both *the Magic of Compound Dreaming* and *the Magic of Compound Vision-Stretching*.

The reason I chose to leave the railroad for ALW was the same reason I would later leave ALW to build WMA—because I had a *clear vision* of what I wanted to accomplish next. When your vision is clear and deeply entrenched in your heart, then you're ready to go all in.

A leader with vision can help their team's dreams come true by making major changes in their life—constantly stretching their vision to include new ways of thinking and new heights to achieve. When a recruit joins and follows us, that's all we're doing. We're stretching their vision and leading them to a new way of life. It's like a rubber band; once you stretch it, it never quite shrinks back to its original size. Becoming the maxed-out version of you doesn't come from just one vision stretching.

CHAPTER 60

OBSESS ON GREATNESS

ONE OF MY PRIMARY GOALS IN WRITING THIS BOOK IS TO CONVEY the importance of being *ALL IN*. I hope that at least one time in your life you can feel what it's like to totally obsess on greatness. I mean being a maniacally dedicated, relentless, laser-focused force of nature that can't and won't be stopped. Someone who gives themselves zero slack and no days off. Someone who is like a freight train powering down the tracks at sixty miles per hour.

That's what Denver was for me. As I've mentioned, I was on the road more than 250 nights a year for four years—recruiting, building, developing leaders, and opening cities. This was my time. I was prepared for this moment. I recognized the importance of the window of opportunity that had opened and I would not be denied.

Like Alexander the Great, I felt like I was in the "grip of a vision" and had a "divine restlessness" driving me. I knew that "genuine empire builders were obsessed and could no more stop following their dream than they could cease to breathe."[24]

My focus as I obsessed on greatness led me to the Volcanic Eruption model wherein we *Surge! . . . Explode! . . . Plateau!* In the same way that volcanic explosions set off a flow of lava that eventually forms mountains, explosive systematic recruiting efforts set off a chain of compound building that eventually leads to large, dynamic teams.

I ran what I called *90-Day Madman Cycles* where I would recruit six to twelve people and produce one to three RVPs. Then, when those ninety days were done, I would repeat and launch into another 90-day cycle. I would break each cycle into three *30-Day Charges* and each Charge into four *Blitz Weeks.* And that's a big part of the secret to my success—the continuous linking of 90-Day Madman Cycles.

The 90-Day Madman Cycle of compressing lots of activity into short, collapsed time frames achieved much more explosive and profitable success than the long, grind-it-out way over an extended period would have.

Think about it like this: If it normally takes you an hour to completely mow your lawn, but you decided to only mow for five minutes each day, it would take you twelve days to mow the whole lawn. By the time you finished, you would have to start mowing again right away. You would never reap the benefit of having a lawn that had been fully mowed. If, however, you mow your lawn in one hour, then you get to enjoy a beautifully manicured lawn until the next mowing.

Using that same principle in recruiting—let's say it takes one hour to recruit one person—it would be much better to invest the twelve hours needed to recruit twelve people (one hour per recruit) during one month rather than recruit one person per month over twelve months. The Mozone power and energy of the crowd of twelve could be harnessed because the duds and the studs all look alike in the beginning. The attrition of the Law of Averages, due to this time compression, would be reduced. My historic twenty-five thousand recruits during the Denver launch occurred over eight consecutive 90-Day Madman Cycles. That's how I went *all in,* building a foundation in twenty-four short months that has lasted for over forty years and has continued with more than 160 consecutive 90-Day Madman Cycles since then.

CHAPTER 61

CONSTANT COURSE CORRECTION

YEARS AGO, I WAS COMPLETELY BLOWN AWAY WHEN I LEARNED that the Apollo 11 spacecraft landed on the moon even though it was off course 90 percent of the time.[25] How was that even possible? The answer: Constant Course Correction.

The Apollo 11 astronauts didn't just aim at the moon and put the rocket on cruise control. In addition to making course corrections themselves while on board the spaceship, the astronauts were in constant contact with mission control and doing exactly what they were told. The launch isn't what was important here, and neither was the landing. What mattered happened during the interim time—during the journey between liftoff and landing. They were course correcting, making precise changes in their trajectory, because a discrepancy of just two or three degrees would have meant missing their mark and ending up on Saturn or beyond! They could only take so much fuel with them on the trip, so it was vital that when they got off course they corrected their pathway as quickly as possible. If they waited too long, they would have used too much fuel.

The astronauts were navigating as if their lives were on the line—because they were. The goal of the mission wasn't to just land on the moon; it was to land on the moon and then return home safely.

Similarly, your business life is always on the line. You're going to be in need of Constant Course Correction because there will always be distractions, interruptions, and errors along the way. I've learned that the real need for a System is to save you from yourself. If you run the System, the System will build and run your business, constantly self-correcting as you go. Then, as a System Leader, all you need is a *Clear Concise Mental Picture (CCMP)* of your destination. When a person joins our business (or starts their own business), they only have a certain amount of fuel (enthusiasm) to use. If mistakes aren't corrected quickly, their enthusiasm will eventually die out and the business will fail. Chances are, like the Apollo astronauts, you'll be *off* course more than *on*, so making the proper corrections is a habit and practice worth adopting. This is why it's so important to have a proven, predictable system to follow.

CHAPTER 62

MAKE YOUR *TOP GUN* AGGRESSIVE VERTICAL MOVE

IN 1986, WHEN THE FIRST *TOP GUN* MOVIE CAME OUT, ONE OF my ALW downline leaders, a retired Air Force officer, gave me a declassified copy of an actual Top Gun manual. The key word that jumped off just about every page was *aggressive*. The message was clear: You can't be a Top Gun pilot without this character- istic. The manual declared that without aggressiveness, all of your other capabilities are useless.

My 90-Day Madman Cycle concept is a great example of what it means to make an aggressive vertical move. I wanted my leaders to be flying around at the equivalent of Mach 2—with their hair on fire! I began the annual tradition of conducting *Top Gun Schools* to help develop future leaders into Top Gun Business Pilots and Business Astronauts.

You can have all the Top Gun training in the world—go to the school, complete all of the simulations—but if you are not willing to fight in the vertical or you do not have the courage to engage the enemy in battle, nothing else matters. Aggressiveness supersedes all other habits, abilities, and skills. In business warfare, aggression fuels victory. I've learned that the best way to maintain aggressiveness is by running our System and building great distribution teams.

CHAPTER 63

SUCCESS IS YOUR BOSS

BECOMING AN ENTREPRENEUR AND BEING THE BOSS OF YOUR own business sounds so romantic, but it can be very deceiving. On the surface it *is* romantic, but at a deeper and more meaningful level, that couldn't be further from the truth. Those who succeed realize that *Success* is their boss. *Success* goes by many aliases: the key alias is *System*. If you run our System, it will help you build and run your business.

Success is a tough boss to work for —it can be mean, nasty, and a heartless taskmaster that will not take any excuse for an answer. Success doesn't care about your past, how you're feeling, where you came from, how much sleep you got last night, or any other excuse you may offer. It's not moved by your politics, whether you're feeling sick, or the balance in your bank account. Success only cares that you do what is required. If you do what Success dictates, you will receive the rewards.

People suffering from one of the main failure diseases, "excusitis," will often come up to me complaining about how certain things can't be done or are seemingly impossible. When they're done pleading their case, I put my finger up to my lips and say, "Shhhhhhhhh! Don't interrupt the people who are already doing what you say can't be done." One of my more effective leadership approaches was showing them a giant-sized baby. I would subtly pull it out and put it on top of my desk.

Success, as a boss, demands things we may not demand of ourselves. I should add here that success doesn't have a human resources department. It doesn't listen to complaints; it doesn't recognize hurt feelings, days off, vacation and sick days, and it doesn't negotiate. Success just knows what must be done, and if those things get accomplished, then it will freely pay out. You must have a passion for your mission, and you must find your *why*. If you don't have a burning desire to do what the System requires, you'll quickly shrink away and fail.

One of my favorite quotes comes from the book *The Greatest Salesman in the World* by Og Mandino. It reads, "I will…leap from my cot while failure sleeps yet another hour."[26] To me, this means that those who answer the call to become successful are willing to be uncomfortable for a time. Mandino continues:

For now is all I have. Tomorrow is the day reserved for the labor of the lazy. I am not lazy. Tomorrow is the day when the weak become strong. I am not weak. Tomorrow is the day when the failure will succeed. I am not a failure…I will act now. Success will not wait. If I delay, she will become **betrothed to another** and lost to me forever. This is the time. This is the place. I am the man. I will act now.

I'll never forget sitting in our big ALW leadership conference in Boca Raton in 1983, when I heard Stanley Beyer, CEO of Penn Corp, make this life-changing statement: "Success, Power, and Wealth are indiscriminate. They don't care who owns them. They are there for whoever thinks they should have them." It struck me like a thunderbolt, almost making me jump up and say, *"Hallelujah!"* in the middle of the meeting.

The bottom line is that the System/Success, as a boss, will give everyone a chance. But are you willing to do what it asks of you, whatever it takes? That's the real question.

CHAPTER 64

A HIGH FQ IS MORE IMPORTANT THAN A HIGH IQ

MANY PEOPLE CARE ABOUT YOUR IQ, YOUR INTELLIGENCE quotient, but I've never been one of them. You could be the smartest person in the room with a hundred different degrees and special awards for your intelligence, and you still wouldn't be able to make it in any of the industries I've succeeded in. I don't care about your IQ. What I care about is your FQ—your failure quotient.

In high school, I was an honor student and a member of the Beta Club. While I was enrolled at Georgia Tech, one of America's top engineering schools, I even made the dean's list the semester before I dropped out. There is a good chance that if I had graduated from Tech, I would have had a good career at a major corporation with a good salary and benefits. Even though I had a decent IQ, ultimately it was my FQ that determined my future. If I'd ended up in the corporate world, none of these business successes I've achieved would have ever happened.

How many times can you fail and keep trying? The answer to this important question can be found in this timeless saying: "It matters not if you try and fail and try and fail again. It matters much if you try and fail but fail to try again." Or, as I like to say, "Can you take a licking and keep on ticking? Can you take a knocking and keep on rocking? If you can just get up one more time than you've been knocked down, you've got a chance!"

Just as you can increase your IQ through studious effort, so can you develop a higher FQ. I have discovered the hard way that the highway to Success runs straight through the city garbage dump. My team lived by the mentality that the harder the blow, the stronger the steel; the harder the times, the more we thrive. Any setback just made us stronger. Thank goodness success doesn't come easy. Because if it did, all the lazy people would have already saturated the market.

CHAPTER 65

THE POWER OF A
MASTERMIND ALLIANCE

ONE OF NAPOLEON HILL'S MOST BRILLIANT INCLUSIONS IN *Think and Grow Rich* was a concept he came up with after a conversation he claims he had with Andrew Carnegie called the *Mastermind Alliance*.[27]

As you know, I have made a career out of studying and imitating successful people. This has helped me to become a critical thinker with the intellectual ability to conceptualize strategic ideas. I have always gleaned from the words and ideas of accomplished and influential leaders. Their thoughts and concepts have become part of my DNA and now belong to me. I highly recommend that you follow this same path to achieve your own success in life. Remember, *you're paid to imitate, not create.*

You don't have to do it alone. Hill found that the most successful leaders had gathered talented teams of people around them. Hill defined this mastermind principle in his book as "a friendly alliance with one or more persons who will encourage one to follow through with both plan and purpose."[28] I copied that principle and surrounded myself with people who knew a lot more than I did to either work with me, work for me, or inspire me from afar. It became the basis for the name of my first company, World Marketing Alliance. I would tell all those who joined us, "You're in business for yourself, but not by yourself." Many of the most important people in my Mastermind Alliance are great historical figures from the past, key business partners, family members, church leaders, and authors of influential books I have read. I am a living example of this promise made by Charlie "Tremendous" Jones: "You will be the same person in five years as you are today except for the people you meet and the books you read."[29] The incredible success that has unfolded in my life and in the lives of my great team leaders is proof indeed that Emerson's words were more than just passing thoughts.

Foremost, I try my best to align myself with Jesus Christ and his apostles, as I study His words and follow His teachings and example. As you have probably already guessed, Alexander the Great was high on my list, as were many great leaders who copied him, such as Napoleon Bonaparte, General George Patton, General Norman Schwarzkopf, and many others. I wasn't interested in becoming a military general, but I was determined to copy their mindsets and apply them to my own life and business pursuits.

I found a kinship with Alexander the Great because I, too, was in the "grip of a vision" and had a "divine restlessness." He lived an extraordinary life and changed the course of human history. He was the beneficiary of his own Mastermind Alliance with the legends of his time. Alexander's father, Philip, sent him to learn from Aristotle at Lyceum, Aristotle's academy. There, Alexander learned about the heroes of *The Iliad*, *The Odyssey*, and other Greek legends. This was when he was inspired to redeem their Greek glory. Aristotle was a student of Plato, and Plato was a student of Socrates. Each learned from one of history's wisest teachers. By going four deep from Socrates to Plato to Aristotle and then to himself, Alexander was able to conquer the known world. This is an excellent example of building a business leg four deep in order to have the best chance of success. Following the leadership principles of someone with such an audacious name as Alexander the Great was exactly what I was looking for. After all, if you're going to emulate someone's best traits, why not choose a person who had indeed conquered the known world?

Alexander's notion of conquering people's hearts is something that I also believe in, as discussed earlier. *If you aim for the heart, the head will follow.* He sold the divided city-states of Greece on the dream of uniting. Thus, by joining his Mastermind Alliance, they would be aligned with something bigger and more powerful than themselves. Alexander the Great wanted to *conquer the world and make it Greek*; and I want to *conquer the world and make it wealthy.*

Some other members of my Mastermind Alliance include:

Napoleon Hill. Hill's book *Think and Grow Rich* was foundational in shaping my mindset.

Andrew Carnegie. Carnegie built his Mastermind Alliance with geniuses. He knew little about the steel industry or about finance, so he surrounded himself with experts in these areas. With this approach, Andrew Carnegie could have dominated any industry at which he aimed his Mastermind Alliance.

Henry Ford. Ford is also a part of my Mastermind Alliance, as he operated the same way as Carnegie.

My mother, June Humphrey. She is probably the greatest influence in my life, even though she died far too early. Her example of mental and emotional strength and discipline is a daily reminder for me to be a better man.

My wife, Norma. I can't say enough about how important she has been in my life. She's my eternal companion, counselor, friend, sweetheart, confidant, and the moral compass that keeps me reined in.

My children, Jody, Kim, Jeffrey, and Jennifer. They have always given me unconditional love and support throughout life's journey.

Art Williams. Art taught me about the crusade and about leadership, and I loved his passion. He was Mr. Outside in the company and Boe Adams was Mr. Inside.

Boe Adams. Boe and I talked constantly, and he really understood me, my role at ALW, and my potential. We were like-minded, and he had my back. With his guidance, I learned many things that were invaluable to me when circumstances later dictated that I leave ALW.

Wood Montgomery. Wood started out as my CPA and evolved into managing my Family Office finances. From there, he became a major part of my strategic Mastermind.

Jim Tenney. Jim has been my personal and corporate general counsel for forty years. He and Wood helped guide me in the building of my great ALW team.

Steve Gross. Steve has been a great friend and strategic business partner during our shared history of over forty years.

Countless others have been a part of my Mastermind Alliance—too many to name here. I suggest you choose people who have the potential to guide you, whether they are historical figures or present-day influences, to be part of your Mastermind Alliance. By the way, I'm happy to be included in that group as well.

During this ALW era, I also compiled a series of important books, which I called my *Success Anthology*. These books helped shape my destiny. Each contained profound principles that collectively served as the foundation for our incredible success.

Think and Grow Rich by Napoleon Hill teaches us the formula for *turning our desires into reality*.

The Magic of Thinking Big by David J. Schwartz teaches us that you don't need a great intellect or great talent to be a giant, but you do need to develop the *habit of thinking bigger* and *acting bigger*.

How to Win Friends and Influence People by Dale Carnegie teaches us that *people don't care how much you know* until they *know how much you care*.

Grinding It Out by Ray Kroc teaches us about the power of *relentless inevitability* that comes from *running a format system*.

The E Myth by Michael E. Gerber teaches us how a *system* can *save us from ourselves* by compensating for any lack that might otherwise prevent us from success.

Waging Business Warfare by D. J. Rogers teaches us the power of *strategic thinking and tactical planning* while making us fully aware that there is a *business war* going on.

The Alexander Complex by Michael Meyer teaches us that the most successful people are driven by a belief in *a mission that potentially will change the course of the world*.

The Mask of Command by John Keegan provides a profile of Alexander the Great's *heroic leadership attributes* so we may copy them and become Modern-Day Alexanders.

Peak Performers by Charles Garfield reveals the common tools *ordinary* people use to achieve *extraordinary* things, including Constant Course Correction.

The True Believer by Eric Hoffer teaches us that once the conditions are right, the *emergence of an outstanding leader* will spark a mass movement.

Made in America by Sam Walton teaches us the enormous benefit of establishing a *partnership* with people as opposed to just being in business with people.

The 7 Habits of Highly Effective People by Stephen R. Covey teaches us how to shift our own *minor* paradigms into more important *major* paradigms.

The Winner Within by Pat Riley teaches us that *teamwork is what makes the dream work.*

In all my businesses, our greatest leaders have applied and taught all of these *Turnkey Success System* principles. The legends of the future must learn from the legends of the past.

Again, I invite anyone who dares to obsess on greatness in life and in business to add me to your Mastermind Alliance.

CHAPTER 66

THE SALE OF ALW TO SANDY WEILL

BY THE TIME 1989 CAME AROUND, I HAD ACCOMPLISHED EVERY-
thing there was to accomplish at A.L. Williams:

- I was the first to make a million dollars in a year.
- I was the first to make two million dollars in a year.
- I was the first to make three, four, and then five million dollars in a year. (There's a trend here!)
- We beat Prudential in 1984.
- I was honored as the Leader of the Decade.
- I produced many generations of millionaire leaders and hundreds of ring earners (recruits making $100,000 or more a year).
- I brought 1.5 million recruits into ALW over a thirteen-year period using my highly effective recruiting and building System, producing over $50 million of income. (In today's terms, using an average $6,000 annual target premium as opposed to the $600 annual target premium back then, that would be over $500 million of income.)
- We sold nearly ten million term policies in thirteen years.
- We changed two major paradigms:
  - The insurance buying habits of Middle America.
  - The insurance selling habits of the life insurance industry.

This all resulted in me earning over six million dollars a year, and it ultimately prepared me to earn several billion dollars of income over the next thirty years in my various other ventures. My plan was to stay with ALW for the rest of my career, but as often happens, life threw me a curve.

In November 1989, I was at a meeting in Toronto with almost three thousand fired-up people eager to hear from me and our leaders. As I was being introduced to a cheering crowd, and before I even started speaking, I was interrupted by the hotel manager. He slipped me a note saying that I was wanted on an emergency call with Art Williams in the manager's office. I brought up Jeff Miles to take over for me and excused myself to go see what was so important that Art needed to interrupt my meeting in Canada.

When I got to the phone, Art and Boe were on the line along with the entire Inner Circle of ALW and Sandy Weill, who, at that time, was the biggest player on Wall Street. They were calling from Sandy's boardroom in New York. I knew something big had to be going on for them to drag me off the stage and to have all these leaders on the call as well. *It was big, alright.* Art announced that Sandy's company, Primerica, had just purchased ALW. You could have heard a pin drop. I couldn't believe what he was saying.

When the call was over, I hung up with a mix of emotions flooding through me: confusion, excitement, shock, and genuine surprise. I really didn't know what it all meant, nor did I grasp the full gravity of the announcement yet, but I knew I was going to stay focused and keep doing what I had been doing. So I gathered myself and went back to my meeting.

No doubt change was coming, but I figured if Art was still in the company, I would be okay. I'd remain single-minded and focused on my team. And I'd continue running the System. I had never contemplated a life after ALW—the thought of leaving simply never crossed my mind. I've always preached that you should align yourself with something bigger than you, and I was perfectly happy to be aligned with ALW and my System. As far as I was concerned, ALW had just aligned with something bigger than itself—new leadership with deeper pockets.

In my view, ALW had only diversified their portfolio with this new alliance. Had they done the things I thought they were going to do, I would probably still be there today. But soon enough, I realized that what I'd heard about Sandy was true. He had a pattern of buying companies and removing the leadership. A few months after Art sold ALW, it was renamed Primerica Financial Services (PFS) and Art was forced out. Of course, when he left, the crusade left with him.

Art's absence created a vacuum, enabling the corporate types to institutionalize the company. In the process, it became a far less inspiring place. I soon discovered that while these new leaders might've understood money, they definitely didn't understand that *heart and soul* is what made ALW such a massive success. And they certainly didn't understand me. I was advised by Sandy's right-hand man that I should stop the "inspirational leadership stuff" and just start managing the team. They asked me to shrink my dreams and bring my vision in line with Sandy's vision.

I couldn't do that. Although the company might have grown stale, corporate, and uninspiring, my team was still on fire and dreaming big dreams. Not only did I not align with management's thinking, but I didn't even know how to. It absolutely blew my mind! I'm not wired that way; it's not in my DNA. My vision had been stretched, and once that happened, it could never go back to the way it was.

No longer could I look a new person in the eye and tell them that if they followed my System as I did, they could get to where I was. And that was what drove me. I had come from nothing and had achieved massive success because of ALW and my System. More importantly, I knew how to make that same thing happen for other driven, determined dreamers. I was in the dream-selling business, and now the company had become traditional and was entrenched in the insurance-selling business.

The passion, the drive, and the crusade of Buy Term and Invest the Difference, which Art had built the company on, evaporated for me. I didn't mind Primerica purchasing ALW. As a matter of fact, I knew we needed deeper pockets, more management, more structure, and more resources. And we certainly needed some heat shields on our rocket ship to protect us from the industry regulators. Historically, it's not unusual for founders, who have taken their company as far as they can, to bring in fresh leadership. Unfortunately, in our case, the new leadership didn't understand the essence of the ALW crusade. Although they would say many of the right things, their words were hollow, and they lacked vision and moral authority.

I went from being focused, happy, and supercharged about our crusade and committed to staying there, to suddenly feeling as if I needed to make a painful decision. I'd be a wild stallion the corporate higher-ups would always try to tame or send to another home.

The legacy of ALW during the thirteen years before it became Primerica is remarkable. Our crusade not only changed the biggest industry in the world, it changed the life insurance buying habits of Middle America. This was a company built to last, and to prove that point, Primerica is still a thriving giant in the industry with a market cap close to $9 billion. I'm proud of what we did at that company, and I'm proud that they are still thriving today. But rising to the challenge of a big idea means you sometimes must leave the safety of your castle walls and risk it all on the battlefield. And that's exactly what I did.

PART THREE

THE SECOND
GREAT CONQUEST
OF THE ODYSSEY:
WORLD MARKETING
ALLIANCE (WMA)

CHAPTER 67

MY GREATEST LEAP
OF FAITH EVER

EARLIER IN MY LIFE I HAD MADE SOME BIG LEAPS OF FAITH. I HAD walked away from Georgia Tech without a degree. Then, with a wife, four children, and a seventeen-year history working for the railroad, I walked away from that income and security. Now, after years of building ALW and achieving all my successes, I was walking away from ALW. This time, however, things were different. The stakes were much higher. I was leaving the company I thought I'd be with for the rest of my career, earning over six million dollars annually, and working with a team that was like my second family. To say that I didn't take leaving ALW/Primerica lightly is an understatement. After a time of being what I would call heartsick, I realized there were no longer any options for a guy like me there, so I made the conscious and willing choice to leave ALW/PFS. This decision came at a great economic risk to myself and my family because I walked away from my source of income and started over from scratch. I loved building teams and being a part of a phenomenal movement. What's more, I never had aspirations to leave or go out on my own. In fact, I would have chosen being a team builder and field leader over being a CEO of a company anytime. It was much more rewarding in every way, but the circumstances didn't leave me any choice. I was ready, the market conditions were ready, the System was always ready, so I pulled the trigger. Failure was not an option.

Where did I get the courage to leave? I'd had my vision stretched while reading *The Alexander Complex*. After my epiphany on the plane, I was ready to rise to the challenge of a big idea—and Alexander, Inc., was a big idea. I felt that I was the sole keeper of the greatest team-building secrets, and I wanted to show the world that I could build an Amway of insurance and mutual funds using my System.

When I left, I thought I had two options. The first option was to align myself with an existing company in the industry and use their resources. The second option was to build a business from scratch. It turned out that the first option wasn't even an option at all. There was nowhere in the industry that could handle the sheer size of my business, recruiting numbers, or production numbers. I was bigger than all of the other companies I looked at. Plus, I was an enigma to the industry—they didn't know what to do with me.

The answer became very clear: I would have to start my own business with the faith that I would find everything I needed. At that point, I had to call my two most trusted financial confidants, Wood Montgomery (my CFO) and Jim Tenney (my general counsel). They both knew that I was very concerned about the ownership changes at ALW, but neither knew that I was ready to make a drastic move. After all, I had just spent millions of dollars on a new mansion and a new jet. When I got them on the phone, I said, *"You're not going to believe what I'm going to tell you... I'm leaving ALW today!"* They knew I was dead serious, so they did the only thing they could do: prepare for battle.

Rising to such a task required that I view all my trials and errors over the years as preparation. I had gone through the refiner's fire and had been tempered. I knew that now I was precisely the right person, in precisely the right place, at precisely the right time, with precisely the right System. I would overcome whatever challenges arose, and I would find a way to win—somehow. I imagined how Alexander the Great would conquer the business world if he were alive today. "His sprawling holding company, Alexander, Inc., would span a dozen advancing technologies, from supercomputers to bioengineering."[30]

And he would keep on doing that until he had conquered it all. I was going to attack my next venture with that same attitude.

CHAPTER 68

ANNOUNCING THE BIRTH OF ALEXANDER, INC.: MY FAMOUS USA TODAY AD

WHEN I LEFT ALW/PFS, I TOLD MY GREAT LEADERS, RICH Thawley, Monte Holm, Jeff Miles, Jack Linder, and Xuan Nguyen, to stay there while I went out to test the waters. I wasn't the type to raid a company upon leaving. I was going to move ahead, and if they wanted to follow me later, that would be up to them. Confident in their own abilities, in me, and in the System, Rich, Monte, and Jeff made their own choice to quickly leave and follow me. Xuan followed shortly thereafter. Some months later, after Jack got through a health issue he had been dealing with, he followed. They, and many others, joined with me to become what I refer to as the original Modern-Day Alexanders. They were my key Warrior Generals, already skilled at building great armies of entrepreneurs.

One reason why I could successfully transition from being a field leader in a company to being the CEO of my own company is because I'd been operating a company within a company for years. In a very real sense, I had been the CEO of my group, Humphrey National Network (HNN), within ALW. In fact, the group became the Humphrey Worldwide Network (HWN) when we expanded to Canada. You will recall the quote in the book *The Alexander Complex*: "His sprawling holding company, Alexander, Inc., would span a dozen advancing technologies, from supercomputers to bioengineering..." Well, that is what I envisioned for us. Thus, the Big Idea took greater shape in my mind. It would be up to me to build a team of Modern-Day Alexanders and give birth to my vision I had conceived during my ALW career, only bigger and better.

As a Do-It-First Leader, I publicly declared my intentions. I spent $150,000 on a full-page ad to appear on the back page of the *USA Today* sports section announcing the birth of my new company, World Marketing Alliance (WMA), a powerful new financial services marketing company delivering variable universal life insurance, term insurance, variable annuities, mutual funds, and more. But most of all, I was still selling dreams.

Over the years, I'd had many more conversations with Boe Adams than I did with Art, because Boe always seemed to understand how valuable I was to the company. He also understood my vision and would nurture and champion me throughout my growth. That's not to say Art didn't appreciate me, but Boe, "Mr. Inside," shared the vision of our team-building system. I studied how he set up the infrastructure of ALW, how he negotiated product contracts, how he set up the commission structure, how he set up meetings, and so forth. I watched and I learned. I attended the company conventions, but I also held conventions of my own.

Given what I had learned from Art and Boe, I was prepared for this moment. With the help of Wood Montgomery and Jim Tenney, I moved forward with the formation of World Marketing Alliance. Several years earlier I had bought a building for my ALW business, which I conveniently converted into our first WMA headquarters in Dunwoody, Georgia. Wood became Executive Vice President and Partner at WMA. Jim continued to be an invaluable strategy and business resource to both Wood and to me directly in the building of WMA. Ten years later, Jim was also heavily involved in the negotiations surrounding the sale of WMA to Aegon.

Not only did we have stellar leaders in the field, but to build a business like we did required a tremendous corporate support team at the headquarters. I had a world-class executive assistant, Susan Davies. She was the hub of our corporate team. She and Judie Fox, my wonderful personal assistant, became indispensable members of my Mastermind group. I have always been blessed, then and now, with a great business family around me.

I could have easily gotten lost in all the details of starting a new company from scratch, but I fanatically focused on the System because I knew it would see us through. As the CEO, I had to find products, construct a home office building, develop compensation structures, deal with employees, and plan and conduct conventions. But as a Do-It-First Leader nothing was more important than modeling how to follow the System. It simply never stops being relevant.

In the great book *Think and Grow Rich*—which compelled me to pursue success back in 1969, and which, not surprisingly, I have referred to several times in these pages—Napoleon Hill lists "Six Ways to Turn Your Desires into Gold." (I quoted the list more fully in chapter 59.) Step 4 reads: "Create a definite plan for carrying out your desire, and begin at once, whether you are ready or not, to put this plan into action." It might seem like I was jumping out of a perfectly good airplane without a parachute, but I had the System, and I knew it worked. Again, I knew I was the right leader, at the right place, at the right time. WMA was the second phase in a continuum that would soon become a great success trilogy, the first phase having been ALW.

CHAPTER 69

THE SECOND ITERATION OF "BUY TERM AND INVEST THE DIFFERENCE"

WHEN STARTING ANY COMPANY, YOU NEED A PRODUCT TO SELL, so one of my first acts was to get the right product line. I had no intention of turning WMA into ALW 2.0. I wanted to diversify our products and bring in licensed industry veterans (in addition to greenies) who were ready to change to our new distribution system. The plan was to aim my System at both the life insurance and securities industries and take them both by storm. Sometime before I left ALW, I was reading an industry trade magazine, *The Best Review*, when I saw an article entitled something to the effect of "The Greatest Product That No One Will Ever Sell." The article discussed a new product called variable life (VL) and variable universal life (VUL), which seemed to be a combination of our Buy Term and Invest the Difference concept and cash value life insurance. I brought it to Boe's attention, but when he said Art had no interest in it, I just filed it away in my brain. I knew it was something to keep an eye on. I was intrigued.

According to the article, there were only a handful of companies that had filed to sell VL and VUL, amounting to just $700 million of premium sold in an industry that measures sales in the trillions. Nine of the top ten industry leaders in this new product category were the usual suspects, including Prudential, New York Life, John Hancock, and other typical mutual companies with captive sales forces. Then, I noticed a company called Western Reserve Life (WRL) near the bottom of the list. They had sold nine million dollars of premium the year before. To put that in perspective, we were doing about nine million dollars of premium *a day* at ALW. I filed this away and knew that at the right time I would contact WRL.

The first product we were appointed to sell was a term life product created specifically for us by Ron Richey at Torchmark Corp., whom I had known for years. The only problem with this product was that it was very expensive.

I knew none of the big companies were likely to talk to me because we had been at war with them for years, so I researched this WRL. I found that they had just been purchased by a big Dutch insurance company, Aegon, with Don Shepard as the CEO of their US division in Baltimore. He told me that I needed to contact Jack Kenney, the newly appointed CEO of WRL. Jack and I hit it off right from the start. He knew all about my crucial role in the historic ALW success.

In fact, Jack had watched our growth with a bit of regret. Turns out that he had been approached by Art years earlier when Art was leaving Waddell and Reed to help start what became ALW. Art was looking for a company to write business with, and he looked to Western Reserve Life and Jack Kenney. WRL had just moved from Ohio to Florida and were not in a position to handle anything with the explosive potential that we had. WRL passed on the ALW opportunity and watched from the sidelines as we took off like a rocket ship. They spent the next thirteen years lamenting that decision. Now Jack, as WRL's new CEO, had another opportunity to work with us in this new WMA company, and he jumped at the chance.

The financial services world was going through major changes at the time. Two industries, life insurance and mutual funds, had been warring and competing for the same client investment assets. It now made sense for them to merge forces because of the 1986 tax law changes, which allowed these new mutual funds' separate account managers to come under the same tax protection as normal cash value insurance policies.

Jack and I discussed the VUL product he had created. When I told him that it looked like a term policy and a mutual fund packaged together, he said that's exactly what it was. He was thrilled that someone finally got it. It was the second iteration of our Buy Term and Invest the Difference crusade. We marketed it as a private pension plan designed for the Baby Boomer generation. In addition to the higher death protection benefit, it now gave us a new crusade focused on *tax advantages of life insurance and the investment advantages of mutual funds.* Legally, it's a type of permanent life insurance that also contains a cash value component that is invested in your choice of multiple sub-accounts (mutual fund–type accounts).

Immediately I saw this as my new flagship product, around which I would build my next great success. I rallied our top fifty original leaders and headed off to meet Jack Kenney and his staff at his headquarters in Clearwater, Florida.

CHAPTER 70

THE BUS RIDE FROM HELL

I RENTED A LARGE EXECUTIVE BUS TO CARRY FIFTY OF MY WMA pioneer leaders on this two-city trip, first to Birmingham, Alabama, to meet with Ron Richey at Torchmark, and then to Clearwater, Florida, to meet Jack Kenney at WRL. We all boarded the bus in Atlanta and began our journey. Traffic that day in Atlanta was legendary as we fought our way to Birmingham. Even though we had several bus problems, we finally made it. After a great meeting with Torchmark, we motored off to Florida. For some reason I thought it was a straight shot from Birmingham to Clearwater, but I quickly learned that we would have to go back through Atlanta and then down to Florida. To further delay us, it became necessary to change buses in Atlanta. It took us all night to get to WRL on a very uncomfortable bus ride.

We rolled into town around five in the morning, which gave us just enough time to freshen up, grab a bite to eat, and then hop back on the bus to go to our meeting with Jack Kenney. Everyone was tired, but we powered through, and the meeting turned out to be one of the most important we'd ever had. Because no one on our team had any prior knowledge of this new product line called VUL, Jack and I really did our best to sell them on it and this new crusade. Although VUL didn't sink in with them at first, that crazy trip turned into a quest and a great memory, which was all part of the price to be paid.

A few days later, I started getting calls from some leaders because they just didn't understand how to sell this new vehicle.

During our time at ALW we'd fought hard against cash value insurance, so some people thought I'd lost my mind and was violating the principles of our initial righteous crusade. Even though teaching this VUL supercharged cash value concept was a hard sell to my team, I finally showed them that we now had our own original Buy Term and Invest the Difference concept inside the wrapper of a cash value policy and were about to beat the industry at their own game. What probably felt to our pioneer group like a bus ride from hell ended up generating a business from heaven.

CHAPTER 71

BEATING THE LIFE INSURANCE INDUSTRY AT ITS OWN GAME

At ALW we always fought against the evils of cash value with its funny banking rules:

1. The insurance company owned your cash value.
2. The insurance company usually only paid about 2 to 3 percent interest on your money.
3. If you wanted to get your cash value out without any penalty, you had to surrender your policy, thus giving up your life insurance coverage.
4. While you could borrow it out as a tax-free loan, they would typically charge you a big interest penalty of 6 to 8 percent.
5. When you died, your cash value became part of the original death benefit.

Now, with Jack's new VUL product, we were able to turn the tables on the industry by using those five cash value funny banking rules to build the perfect tax-free personal retirement plan for Baby Boomers:

6. The fact that the insurance company owned the cash value is what gave it its tax-free status.
1. Now your return was determined by the performance of the mutual fund's separate account manager in the stock market, which, during our WMA era, was averaging

well in excess of 10 to 12 percent, and in some periods, much higher.

7. This way, you could get your cash value out without penalty and be able to keep your death protection.

8. The cash value loan provision, where you could borrow it out at a percentage at a 6 to 10 percent penalty on the loan, actually provided the perfect withdrawal method. But this time, there was something called a *zero wash loan,* which was actually a subsidy credit. For example, if you took out a loan of your cash value at 6 percent interest, there was a 6 percent subsidy credit from the separate account funds that zeroed out the 6 percent cash value loan interest penalty rate, permitting you to withdraw it tax-free as long as you didn't surrender the policy. Now you had the perfect scenario, "Tax-free withdrawal on tax-free cash retirement accumulations with fund managers."

9. Upon death, the beneficiary received the full face amount of the insurance death protection and the full amount of the fund account as the combined death protection.

To break the ice and stretch everyone's vision regarding VUL, I knew I had to have a big kickoff meeting. I called Jack Kenney and asked him if he had anyone who made a million dollars a year selling VUL. I needed someone to come train us and show the team that big money could be made by selling this product. He said, "Actually, I do have an advisor who has made over a million dollars selling VUL, and he lives not far from you in Athens, Georgia. But he's a tough guy to deal with." I replied, "If he's made a million dollars, then he's my kind of guy."

When I contacted him, he was a little hesitant at first. He still saw me as a competitive threat to WRL and didn't fully understand the magnitude of the ALW crusade. He had a healthy ego, so I had to brag about him and build him up before he finally let his guard down enough to listen. I told him what I was planning and that I would love someone like him to speak with our team. After our initial phone conversation, I had my staff create a flier about this revolutionary new concept and opportunity. It promoted me as The Babe Ruth of Building and Recruiting and a Multimillion Dollar Earner, and him as the Babe Ruth of VUL and a Million Dollar Earner. He really liked the sound of The Babe Ruth of VUL. That was exactly what his ego needed. From then on, we made magic together.

The meeting was a great success; the concept of VUL as the second iteration of the Buy Term and Invest the Difference made sense to our team. Our WMA slogan became *Tax Advantages of Life Insurance with the Investment Advantages of Mutual Funds*.

I look back and marvel at the timing of everything—how all the conditions were perfect for our success. WRL had been sold a few times, the leadership was getting tired of it, and they were even considering doing something else. Jack Kenney had just been appointed CEO and was frustrated that he couldn't get many people from his old team to see the power of the VUL concept. As fate would have it, their product was perfect for a team like ours.

WMA would go on to disrupt and redefine the industry just as we had done at ALW. Over the next ten years we recruited over five hundred thousand new agents and sold more than five million VUL policies, producing $350 million in VUL premium! We changed the investing habits of Middle America while cementing the merging of the insurance and mutual fund industries. The fact that this was the first time in their world that advanced annualized commissions were paid on the submission of a securities-based product was another monumental way we changed the securities industry. This was revolutionary.

CHAPTER 72

THE INDUSTRY WAS ASLEEP AT THE WHEEL...AGAIN!

SELLING VUL, "THE GREATEST PRODUCT THAT NO ONE WILL Ever Sell," was a challenge for everyone in the industry—except us. Here's the industry's dilemma: This powerful new VUL product required both a sales force of dually-licensed sales agents and high-volume production to be profitable. That's right, a life insurance license and a securities license were both necessary to sell this product, but no one in the industry had a field force with enough dually-licensed people. This is how asleep at the wheel the industry was—93 percent of insurance agents didn't have a securities license, and 99 percent of securities agents didn't have an insurance license. Enter Hubert Humphrey and his army of disrupters, having thirteen years of experience at ALW building a giant dually-licensed army.

With our Buy Term and Invest the Difference crusade at ALW, the Invest the Difference part meant the client should invest in mutual funds so their money could grow for retirement. Selling mutual funds required a securities license. We were the only company that had any kind of experience getting a field force dually licensed. We knew how to do it. One of the weaknesses in the ALW philosophy was that the insurance and mutual funds were unbundled, and many people didn't have the discipline to actually save the difference that was freed up. VUL took care of that. It was *prepackaged discipline* for the client.

These products had been created as a reaction to the tremendous replacement success of ALW. When I saw that the new products required agents to be licensed in both insurance and securities, I knew that our thirteen years of building a dually-licensed army of over one hundred thousand crusaders positioned us to totally dominate a divided industry once again.

Prudential had spent the last thirteen years being beaten up by ALW, so they wanted to be prepared against it happening again. Around the time Art sold ALW, Prudential saw the emerging market for variable life (VL) products and used Bache, a company they had purchased earlier, to build a field force of thirty thousand dually-licensed agents futilely hoping to protect their dominant position.

I knew aiming my recruiting and building system of selling dreams at this new market would create the second great financial revolution.

There is nothing quite like the feeling of being in the right place at the right time and knowing that you are 100 percent prepared for the opportunity. That was WMA. It was a more powerful earning vehicle than ALW. We were able to produce more business and earn more money per recruit. We went on a run of recruiting, selling, and creating wealth for families that was unbelievable. With this new VUL product in hand, we overtook the industry, beating Prudential again, changing the way insurance and securities were sold, and introducing a whole new delivery system for these new products.

VUL was such a powerful product for the client, and it paid well. At ALW, clients were paying $500–$600 in annual target premium. At WMA, a client would pay $1,500–$2,000 in annual target premium. This meant our agents were being paid much more per transaction with VUL than they were with term insurance. That's why WMA outproduced ALW in annual premium with less than half the agents during a shorter time period. This, still, was only just the beginning of our incredible odyssey of building three multibillion-dollar market cap companies.

CHAPTER 73

THE SYSTEM WHEREBY RECRUITING AND BUILDING NEVER STOPS

As the CEO of WMA, I knew the System would be my salvation. When you are starting a business from scratch, dealing with the minutiae could cost you everything. You have an onslaught of details to attend to in order to implement all the things you took for granted in your old, well-established place. I could have easily been derailed. But as a Do-It-First Leader, nothing was more important than modeling how to follow the System, so I put my attentions there.

I preached following the System until I was blue in the face. I preached it until my team was tired of hearing it. But I had to do it. A system is essential and exactly what new entrepreneurs need. I taught repeatedly that *the rapid, relentless repetition of the System's Six Simple Recruiting Steps and Eight Filters can lead to an inevitable explosion.*

Now, more than ever, I had to stay focused on teaching my old and new leaders the System. A system simply imposes a new set of success habits that would *save them from themselves* and all of life's distractions. That's it. Having a System not only allowed me to succeed and disrupt an entire industry, but it also leveled the playing field for anyone else who wanted to suit up and get in the game. With a System to follow, anyone could succeed regardless of age, gender, ethnicity, race, or income.

CHAPTER 74

THE LEADERS OF WMA

As mentioned earlier, a short time after I left ALW and started WMA, several of my key leaders—Rich Thawley, Monte Holm, Xuan Nguyen, Jeff Miles, and Jack Linder—took the bold step of joining me in this great new undertaking. Having distinguished themselves as Super Team leaders and builders in our ALW era, they became the key foundational leaders of this historic new company.

Rich and Cindy were at the forefront of my Inner Circle. Rich was instrumental in helping to develop our greatest WMA leader of all time, Xuan Nguyen, who built the Nguyen dynasty into the largest and most productive team in financial services. As my chief business disciple from ALW, Rich had the moral authority to be the master business model and the teacher of our Leadership Format System for our great new company.

Monte and his wife and partner, Lisa, built the Holm empire into one of WMA's greatest business teams. Monte was one of my great wingmen, and his leadership was invaluable.

Jeff and his wife and partner, Debbie, were among my most valuable Field Generals and Super Team builders helping us expand nationally, and they were extremely helpful to us in opening WMA of Canada.

Jack and Linda Linder also helped us build some of the great Super Teams in WMA. Jack, too, was another of my great wingmen.

Tom and Cindy Mathews later joined our Inner Circle of Champions, building great leadership teams such as Bill and

Peggy Mitchell's. Tom was invaluable as he prepared us for the internet era and the use of all the new technology tools. I had known Tom back in the ALW days, though he had been with a different team. Tom had a degree of success at ALW, but he left sometime after Art sold the company, hoping to start his own financial services business. Tom was a smart and resourceful guy and, back then, would be classified as an "entrepreneurial geek."

When Tom realized the success we were having at WMA, running our System and marketing this powerful new variable universal life product, he quickly joined us. He brought a unique set of talents to our company. In addition to being a good leader and team builder, his aptitude for technology would play an important role in our future. Tom and Cindy moved from Cincinnati to Atlanta to not only build a great team, but to be a part of my Mastermind Alliance, especially in the area of technology. Still today, Tom is one of the stalwart leaders in the industry.

Bryce Peterson played a great role in the development of WMA, too, especially as he grasped the power of the VUL product and led his team to become our top producers in 1991.

Jody Humphrey came over with us right away and aligned himself under the leadership of Rich Thawley to become one of our Super Team leaders and Warrior Generals. Jody's team-building experience at ALW, and the lessons he learned growing up as my eldest son, helped him become one of our most valuable leaders.

Now I come to Xuan and Hoa Nguyen. I saved Xuan for the end of this chapter to highlight him, because he stands alone. He became the leader of the Nguyen dynasty, one of the greatest financial services teams ever built. He stood above everyone as the preeminent Warrior General. Once he mastered the System, he never faltered. He ran it better than any other leader I have known, even to this day.

Because of the language barrier, it took some time for Xuan and his leaders to get their securities licenses, but they more than made up for the delay. Earlier in the book, I said that the First System Engine is to have a Recruiter's Mentality. Let me illustrate why that is so important with a story about Xuan.

While most people in the company were focused on learning about this new product, which was important, Xuan knew that it was even more important to never stop recruiting. He didn't panic during those early months when others were passing him by in production and cash flow. He knew that while he and his team were figuring out the licensing issues, they were continuously recruiting and building a great team. He was confident that they would be ready for a production explosion as soon as they were all securities-licensed. And that's exactly what happened. They shot to the top of the company and never looked back. Xuan was focused on the right things—*recruiting, building, motivation*—even as he was learning challenging new things.

This story perfectly describes Xuan's mentality. During World War II, Winston Churchill was the prime minister of England overseeing the war effort. At a pivotal time in the fighting, he received an urgent letter from a beleaguered general who was under heavy siege, requesting reinforcements. Churchill wrote back and gave two direct orders:

Direct Order No. 1: "Organize and succeed at all costs."

Direct Order No. 2: "There will be no further orders."

Likewise, I gave my leaders only two direct orders:

Direct Order No. 1: "Build leaders and teams will come."

Direct Order No. 2: "There will be no further orders."

While others were majoring in minor things, Xuan and his leaders remained focused on my Direct Order No. 1 and Direct Order No. 2.

The Nguyen Dynasty's rise was the preeminent driving force in the growth of the great WMA phenomenon. Xuan followed the principles of my Leadership Format System exactly, helping him build great leaders and teams. He followed these three System Engines: Recruiter's Mentality, Builder's Mindset, and Director of Motivation.

Over the course of his career, Xuan and his wife and partner, Hoa, have earned over a half billion dollars. Not bad for a refugee from the Vietnam War, who started in America as a social worker, speaking very little English and having no business or insurance industry training. Remember that it all started because he accidentally walked into the wrong office back in our early ALW days, and someone led with the opportunity and sold him the dream.

It only takes a small spark to ignite a great future.

CHAPTER 75

THE SALE OF WMA TO AEGON: DUPLICATING THE SAME SUCCESS PATTERN

WITH THE HELP OF ALL THESE EXCEPTIONAL LEADERS, WE GREW to great heights and achieved phenomenal success. We had done what we set out to do.

We had paid out over a billion dollars in commissions to our sales force and several billion dollars of protection and wealth to their clients. We had disrupted not only the insurance industry again, but with the VUL product, we had also disrupted the securities industry. We had beaten Prudential once again and were recognized as national champions for the second time.

In that historic ten-year span, we produced approximately...

- Five hundred thousand recruits
- Over $5 million sales
- Thousands of ring earners (team members making in excess of $100,000 annually)
- Dozens of million-dollar cash flow leaders
- Crowds of nearly twenty-eight thousand attendees at our conventions featuring celebrity speakers and performers.

The phenomenal growth and success of WMA exceeded our wildest expectations. By marketing VUL and VA, we were able to produce more commissionable premium in ten years than we did marketing Buy Term and Invest the Difference in the course of thirteen years at ALW. Just as they sold ALW after thirteen years of meteoric growth to Sandy Weill's new company (soon to be called Citigroup), renaming it Primerica, we sold WMA after ten phenomenal years to WRL's parent company, Aegon, who renamed it World Financial Group (WFG).

This was set into motion after we struck our original deal with WRL and agreed that it would be best if we became an affiliate of Aegon. Aegon had watched the growth of ALW and its sale to Citigroup and decided they wanted to be positioned to buy us if and when the time was right. We were now producing almost 50 percent of the profits of Aegon USA. For years, Aegon wanted to buy WMA in a stock transaction, but I knew there was more growth to be had, and we just weren't ready. I had learned from ALW that at some point WMA would need to be aligned with something bigger than itself. So, I would sell, but only when the conditions were ideal.

When indeed the time finally came to sell the company to Aegon, I recalled Art's regret that he had taken most of his Citigroup payment in stock, because it proved to be very volatile for him. Similarly, Aegon wanted to do a stock deal with me, but I chose an all-cash deal instead. I'm grateful I did that because about forty-five days after our deal closed, the terrorist attacks of September 11, 2001, occurred. It was one of the darkest days in our nation's history. Needless to say, the markets were negatively impacted.

Aegon's stock had historically been strong, but in early 2000, even before 9/11, the market started to show signs of slowing. Then in October 2002, still in the wake of the dot-come bubble's burst, the stock market took a major dive, reducing Aegon's stock value by almost 75 percent.

At the close of our sale to Aegon, I distributed almost $40 million from the proceeds to over two hundred of our key leaders who helped us build WMA. *Promises made, promises kept.*

I am so proud of WMA, now known as World Financial Group or WFG, and its built-to-last legacy. With a more than $7 billion market cap value within the publicly traded Aegon company, it continues to be a thriving player in the industry.

By the end of 2002, knowing that I had left our leaders well prepared and in good hands, I exited the company and readied myself for my next business venture. I was headed into the mortgage and real estate world. Little did I realize that the great recession of 2008 was on its way, illustrating, once again, the importance of having a safety net like a life insurance—centric business to fall back on.

CHAPTER 76

THE GREAT INTERRUPTION

WHEN I SOLD WMA TO AEGON, I SIGNED A TEN-YEAR NONCOM-
pete agreement in the insurance field. I was free to build any
business I wanted as long as I wasn't heading up an insurance organization. Unbelievably, Aegon chose not to include
in the purchase some very important assets, such as WMA
Canada (WMAC), WMA Investment Advisory (WMAIA),
WMA Coinsurance Company, and WMA Mortgage (WMAM).
So, I took WMAM and WMAIA and aimed our foolproof,
predictable, and duplicatable System there. With the mortgage window being so wide open, I saw this as part of the
Economic Inevitability of the financial market situation. I
knew we were in the right place at the right time to enter this
new industry. I named the new company World Leadership
Group, Inc. (WLG), and it took off. We ran our recruiting
and building System, but this time in the world of mortgages,
real estate, and assets under management. Even though I was
still under an extended noncompete, I launched an insurance
agency hoping to renegotiate my agreement with Aegon. I had
wanted to use it as a safety net. When they refused my request,
I had to continue to comply with my noncompete; however, I
later outsourced this company to an outside investor. In fact,
that little insurance company grew over time into an entirely
separate insurance marketing company, known today as First
Financial Security (FFS).

With our System at WLG now focused primarily in the
mortgage business, we recruited almost two hundred thousand

people and became the number one originator of loans for some of the biggest companies in the industry: Countrywide, Washington Mutual, Flagstar, World Savings, and others. We led with the dream and opportunity, aimed for the heart, and knew the head—and production—would follow. At our peak, we were originating between fifteen thousand and eighteen thousand loans a month. But we remained a dream-selling, team-building company marketing mortgages instead of insurance, as we had done in previous companies.

At WLG, we were making more money in the mortgage business per transaction than we ever made in the insurance business. Now my System was working at a third great company and in a third major industry. Instead of Buy Term and Invest the Difference, we were selling Refinance and Invest the Difference. With products like adjustable-rate mortgages (ARM), the trajectory of WLG started off better than ALW and WMA at the same time in their histories. Even while I was building WLG, I knew I would end up back in the insurance world after my noncompete expired. But the clock ran out before I could get back into that game. We were in talks with Countrywide, the mortgage industry leader, for a possible sale of our company to them that would have exceeded our WMA sale to Aegon. But in 2007, after signs of a serious slowdown in the industry emerged, that prospect ended. By 2009, the bottom dropped out as, suddenly, the world was in a global systemic financial meltdown. No one was loaning money anymore.

I learned a painful lesson during this time: Windows of opportunity can close just as quickly as they can appear. That's what happened as our window closed almost overnight. One day, we were a dominant player in the mortgage world; the next day, companies like Washington Mutual were closing their offices nationwide. This led to the Great Recession when Baby Boomers lost 75 percent of their net worth. It was a fiasco.

Our Leadership Format System didn't fail; the global economy did. The systemic worldwide economic meltdown was a result of several factors: the government completely messing up Fannie Mae and Freddie Mac; Wall Street, the global banks, and global financiers newly and greedily marketing mortgage-backed securities; and a lot of big lenders pushing profit-rich subprime loans. (If you could fog a mirror, you could get a loan without proof you could pay it back!) For the record, we never sold even one subprime loan—only "A" paper. Under these conditions the industry collapsed, catching me without the insurance company safety net I had been prohibited from building because of the noncompete.

Coupled with the fact that I had poured millions into building WLG, invested millions more into various investments—such as real estate ventures, banks, and our fifty-thousand-square-foot mansion on ninety acres—I made the strategic decision to do three things:

1. I shut down WLG. I simply remembered the Law of Holes: *When you find yourself in a hole, quit digging.* It's kind of like I was now facing a negative economic inevitability.
2. I drew up a financial plan to clean the slate and eliminate debts through liquidation and Chapter 11 bankruptcy, thus preparing for my next great move.
3. I prepared to reenter the life insurance business by building my third great financial services company as soon as my noncompete with Aegon ended.

Fortunately, throughout this difficult time, I was reminded of the unwavering faith that Norma and my family had in me.

PART FOUR

THE THIRD GREAT CONQUEST OF THE ODYSSEY: HEGEMON GROUP INTERNATIONAL (HGI)

CHAPTER 77

THE GREAT RESUMPTION

MY DREAM OF BUILDING *ALEXANDER INC., THE BIG IDEA* WAS STILL alive and, as you'll soon see, would manifest in the form of Hegemon Group International (HGI), the fourth major part of our great odyssey.

While these were unprecedented times, I actually had some practice at starting over. You will recall that during the last eight years of my railroad career, I had given up half of that income to pursue my Amway dream. When I finally joined ALW, not only did I give up the security that seventeen years of seniority on the railroad afforded me, but I also gave up my eight-year parallel career at Amway.

After ALW was sold, again I left security and prosperity behind. I said goodbye to the team I had built over thirteen years—fifty thousand licensed agents strong—and an income upwards of $6 million dollars annually, as well as future renewal income that, if I had stayed, would have paid me anywhere between $300 million and $400 million (equal to over $2 billion dollars in today's market) over the next three decades.

During the four years of the Great Interruption and following the suspension of my WLG mortgage and real estate company, I spent my time waiting for my noncompete to expire and preparing for the Great Resumption—the building of my third revolutionary, multibillion-dollar insurance marketing company. There were two things I was absolutely sure of: the *predictability* of my Leadership Format System; and the *Circle of Safety* and *Economic Inevitability* that the life insurance industry provided. It was the ultimate safety net I had missed having during those high-wire years at WLG. I wouldn't make that mistake again. The life insurance industry is recession proof, inflation proof, government proof, even pandemic proof. It's also self-replicating, self-financing, and self-training. The next company was going to, once again, be built on these five M's: Multiples, Motivation, Money Products, Machines, and Market Conditions.

I'd learned a lot of hard lessons, but at no point did I consider myself or our System a failure. The Great Recession was an unforeseen, once-in-a-lifetime, systemic global melt-down that was not of my making. But, if life has taught me anything, it's that just as some windows close, others will open. That very Trying Motor that got me going in the beginning was still very much running. Now, more than ever, was the time to be a Do-It-First Leader, to keep dreaming, and to surround myself with the right people. Success was still my boss. I knew what it demanded. And I was ready to pay the price to succeed again.

I downsized my life, battened down the hatches, and put a plan together to get through the next few years of my noncompete. Then, in 2014, I launched Hegemon Group International (HGI), which would become my third multibillion-dollar market cap company. While we were bootstrapping and waiting for the time to reenter the life insurance world, we marketed several referral-based alternative investment products such as land banking, which allowed us to recruit and bring in cash flow. I was able to secure our initial strategic investors. Shortly thereafter, Steve Gross became an investor and perfect partner as we went on to build the great success that we have today. Steve has been that invaluable inside Mastermind ally to me, just as Boe Adams was to Art Williams, and just as Wood Montgomery was to me in the building of WMA. Jim Miller is another key person who I really must pay tribute to here. He has played an important role in my success as my personal and company banker for the last forty years and was one of the key investment partners in HGI.

CHAPTER 78

THE CONTINUUM OF "THE BIG IDEA"

EVER SINCE I READ *THE ALEXANDER COMPLEX* BACK IN THE 1980S, I have been on a mission to build my vision of Alexander Inc., The Big Idea. It has always been *the big idea* that drove me. The business lessons learned selling dreams at Amway combined with the experience of selling multiples and money products while building leadership teams at ALW and WMA (respectively, the first and second acts of my financial services odyssey) set the stage for us building HGI (the third act of my financial services odyssey). And true to the form of a heroic story, the transition from act two to act three came at a high cost. But I persevered, and this fourth act of my business story would prove to be the greatest of them all.

When HGI began, we once again enjoyed the greatest window of demographic and economic inevitabilities yet. The US population had increased by over one hundred million since the start of ALW. Much of this was attributed to two important immigration trends: the explosive growth of the Hispanic population—the fastest-growing ethnic group in the US; and the dynamic influx of the Indian population—the most affluent ethnic group in the country.

Then, as now, people were dreaming and wanting more out of life. These new groups migrating to the United States were uniquely prepared for this window of opportunity. The stage was set for the birth of HGI. As recruits, these hardworking, educated, and driven people became a major force in our company and in the industry. So many leaders and teams have emerged, rising from having fully embraced the System and realizing incredible results.

CHAPTER 79

COPY THE LEGENDARY TEAM BUILDERS OF THE PAST

ANOTHER PRINCIPLE I HAVE TAUGHT REPEATEDLY FOR DECADES IS *Build Leaders and Teams will Come.* I've seen this play out time and time again.

We have built Driven, Determined Dreamers who run our System correctly, creating tremendous new entrepreneurial growth in all of the US population, especially in the Indian, Asian, and Hispanic groups.

These new leaders we're currently developing at HGI are as powerful and have as much potential as any I've ever been associated with. Combine my proven System with the power of the industry, the transference of wealth that is happening, and the quality of people we are bringing in, and we are, once again, blasting through new windows of opportunity. As the Baby Boomers enter their retirement years, other massive demographic oceans of people are rising in their wake. The invitation is for you to join us in the building of leaders and teams in this next great chapter of success.

Earlier in the book, I wrote that *The First Principle of Leadership is Followership.* For the leaders of today to become the legends of the future, they must relentlessly copy the legends of the past. That is exactly what has happened at HGI. I have watched countless people follow our proven and predictable System, becoming wildly successful in the process.

Let me share an example. At ALW, I established the proto-type of the perfect System. This prototype became the master copy. Later, as Rich Thawley emerged, he duplicated my example exactly and became our greatest leader. You could say he was a mini-me. He ate, drank, and slept the System. Then, by copying Rich's example, Xuan Nguyen became the dominant leader at WMA/WFG and is still a major force in that business. Now at HGI, Akki Roopani has taken up the mantle of the new prototypical System leader and builder of this era. He has a chance to become our greatest of all time.

CHAPTER 80

A WHOLE NEW GENERATION
OF HGI SUPER-LEADERS

WE ARE CREATING A WHOLE NEW GENERATION OF FUTURE leaders who are copying the legends of the past. They are building bigger, better, and faster than ever before.

The System puts the Law of High Numbers into effect, making the Law of Averages profitable. Ultimately our success comes down to *lots of people doing a little bit and a few doing a lot*. Run the System, and the System will sort the leaders out. Finding great leaders such as Akki and his wonderful wife, Ronak Roopani, one of the great power couples in financial services history, is proof of that philosophy.

Three years and several thousand recruits after the launch of HGI, a great new window of opportunity opened when I met Akki. He had been with WFG (previously WMA before I sold it to Aegon) for about four years.

Akki had left India to come to America, where he took a management position with a New York company. After some time, he settled in Atlanta, where he ran a chain of service stations. Along the way he was introduced to the WFG opportunity, getting into the financial services business. When he saw the tremendous financial potential it offered, he was greatly intrigued. Upon joining WFG he immediately immersed himself in learning all that he could about the life insurance and annuity industry, using YouTube tools and WFG's training programs.

During that four-year period, Akki developed his first four or five strong, foundational leaders and a team of over four hundred agents. He also built his income up to around $400,000 per year. But WFG's version of my Leadership Format System was limited. He had an increasing desire to learn the System secrets Xuan Nguyen and other fine leaders had learned from me. This was, in fact, his motivation to join me in my new venture at HGI—to duplicate the Master Copy directly from the original architect of the System.

After hearing that Akki wanted to talk to me, I gave him a call. It's amazing to think about the effect such a simple little phone call would have on the arc of our business history. Shortly after that conversation, Steve Gross, Jody Humphrey, and I met with Akki and a handful of his key leaders, including Prashant Morajkar and Shawn Sadruddin. After Akki and Ronak made the decision to join HGI, Prashant and Madhuri Morajkar, Shawn and Rozina Sadruddin, and several other of their key leaders, including Bhagwan and Supraja Reddy, Srinivas and Latha Maram, Raghu and Jyothi Reddy, Thiru Reddy, Reshma and Salim Hajiyani, and Altaf and Minisha Hemdani, soon joined and have all now become multimillion-dollar per year earners.

Akki and Ronak have become the flagship leadership team at HGI, in the same way that Norma and I were at ALW and Xuan and Hoa were at WMA. These powerful new System disciples are great at team building and at product and financial education training.

In six short years, Akki has broken all of our team-building and production records and is rewriting the history books. His income has grown to over $10 million a year, and he is expected to achieve $20 million in the next twelve months. He and his great team are destined to be our biggest and best ever.

Not only that, but during the last two or three years, several more million-dollar earners have emerged on Akki's team, among them Preethi and Sai Munagapati, Pratik and Jaya Rashingkar, Ravik and Rupa Vinjamuri, Kandasamy and Chitra Subburaj, Yugi and Sabitha Dontam, Ravi and Hema Somisetty, Rahim and Hiral Hussain, Dr. Jayesh and Rita Patel, Saurbah and Tulika Puri, Zaheer and Sameera Gillani, Samina and Shiraz Ismail, Tejas and Akta Patel, and several more rapidly rising leaders.

Also, under the incredible leadership of Jody and Crisabeth Humphrey, a whole new leadership generation of million-dollar earners has emerged. Jody is using his vast leadership experience, which he garnered over the past forty years observing various legends at our great companies. Here are just a few of these special new rising stars: Mauricio and Lorena Garcia, Rafael and Tatiana Preciado, Francisco and Silvia Marquina, Humberto Luongo, Stephanie and Breetzy Pinto, Rory and Andrea Douglas, Zack and Kimberly Otey, Rafael Garcia, James Ivanovich, Sergio and Rosangela Villegas, and Greg Smith—with many more on the way.

All of the great leaders mentioned in this chapter have a common thread of success; they share a *Passion for our Mission and a Submission to our System.* They are examples of how using a predictable, foolproof, duplicatable, profitable system works. Combining a system like ours with multiples and money products has always produced *thermonuclear* opportunities.

Our HGI Mission Statement is *Creating Wealth for Families.* You can see the growth and power in this trilogy of great companies by looking at the commission payout to the field in each company.

- ALW paid out more than a billion dollars in commissions to the field in a fourteen-year period.
- WMA paid out more than a billion dollars in commissions to the field in a ten-year period.
- HGI is on target to pay out more than a billion dollars in commissions to the field in only a seven-year period.

As we complete the three-year earnout from the sale of HGI to Integrity in 2025 (more about that in the next chapter), we are on track to potentially reward our top-qualifying leaders in the accumulation of equity share credits with a portion of the proceeds from the sale.

These are just a few of the examples of *Promises Made, Promises Kept* to our entrepreneurial field force and their tremendous client base.

CHAPTER 81

CONTINUING THE PATTERN OF SUCCESS: HGI ALIGNS WITH INTEGRITY MARKETING GROUP (IMG)

THE EXPERIENCE I'VE GATHERED OVER THESE DECADES AND OUR ability to align ourselves with something bigger than ourselves has led to a new partnership with Integrity Marketing Group (IMG). Truly, the future has never looked brighter.

We built our two previous organizations to grow, last, and succeed as world-class companies. With that in mind we have now aligned with the formidable Integrity to provide a solid succession plan and a better fit with the modern competitive world. Integrity's shared services platform offers our professional advisors and their valued clients an unlimited diversified array of financial products, solutions, tools, and services with which to perform at a best-in-class level.

This commitment to aligning ourselves with such world-class partners has contributed to our success with all our previous multibillion-dollar companies:

- At ALW, we aligned with Primerica Financial Group (which later became Citigroup).
- At WMA, we aligned with Aegon.
- At HGI, we have now aligned with Integrity Marketing Group (IMG).

Integrity's platform page says it all: "Integrity is a one-of-a-kind company that uses technology, data, and a human touch to deliver a better insurance and financial services experience. We innovate in ways that help people protect their life, health, and wealth holistically. So, they can make the most of what life brings."

Finding the right partner at the right time has been a key to our success, resulting in more reach, money, resources, technologies, and relationships than we could have ever secured on our own. Our alignment with IMG also provides regulatory and financial protections, products, and other strengths that help to ensure our longevity. What's more, our great entrepreneurial team builders can potentially sell their income streams to IMG for a large earnings multiple as a Managing Partner with the prospect of sharing in IMG's growth potential.

Our crusade is more powerful than ever. The evolution from Buy Term and Invest the Difference to *variable universal life* (VUL) has now matured to *indexed universal life* (IUL), *indexed annuities* (IA), and *assets under management* (AUM).

We are in a much more powerful position to help people from all walks of life, including people like you, to *conquer your future* by *gathering teams under professional leadership* and *gathering assets under professional management*. An army of money will eventually outproduce an army of leaders because, as Gordon Gecko famously said in the movie *Wall Street*, "Money never sleeps, pal."

Now more than ever, this great quote about Alexander the Great applies to us:

> After four years with an army, Alexander made himself master of a power whose extent and speed of acquisition stand unequaled before or since. In 330 BC, he had only to follow up his third crushing victory to

be acknowledged ruler of lands that covered a million square miles.

He had become many thousand times richer than anyone else in his world. He began as king of the Macedonians and confirmed himself as master of the Greeks, Pharaoh of Egypt, and by conquest, the King of Asia. But he had no intention of stopping. A year earlier, he had asked an oracle of the gods in the Libyan desert which deities he should honor when he reached the Outer Ocean. The ocean, he believed, was the edge of the world. Already, he aimed to conquer everything until the world ran out.[31]

My goal is to stretch the vision of all you Modern-Day Alexanders, duplicating my desire and preparation to conquer whatever is next. I consider HGI my third crushing victory. I want you to understand: I still have the drive, the vision, and the relentlessness that it takes to "conquer everything until the world runs out."

CHAPTER 82

GIVE YOUR EFFORTS ENOUGH TIME TO COMPOUND

LET ME REMIND YOU THAT, IF IT HAD BEEN POSSIBLE, I WOULD have chosen to be a field leader, the way Xuan Nguyen and Rich Thawley are at WMA/WFG, with all of the right resources for success at my disposal, rather than start my own company. Knowing what I know now, if it had been possible to have the right diversification of products, I would have much preferred staying in the *right place* (ALW), having learned the *right System*, from the *original copy*, staying in the same company the whole time.

My ego is not what caused me to leave ALW and build other companies. I had never planned to strike out on my own, but when ALW was sold, it was no longer a place conducive to me or my team's growth, especially with its myopic focus on the sale of only term insurance. I had to leave and create a better environment for myself and thousands of others to succeed.

When WMA/WFG was established, it was a place where people could flourish and achieve unlimited financial success as they gave their efforts enough time to compound. What's more, they had been taught how to successfully run our powerful Leadership Format System. For these reasons, I challenge people to get in the right place with a great system and be successful there.

The ALW/PFS opportunity was the greatest opportunity for its time during the 1980s. WMA/WFG was an even greater opportunity for its time during the 1990s. Now, HGI is poised to be the greatest opportunity of them all in the 2020s. Today, HGI is the right place at the right time, because today you have the Master Copy—the architect of the System itself. You also have a full array of products and provider relationships. And you're aligned with Integrity Marketing Group, one of the largest financial services companies in the world.

The odds are that almost 99 percent of leaders who leave a successful entrepreneurial environment like ours to start their own businesses will fail. And I can tell you from firsthand experience that you will most likely net out far more money with a system like ours than if you invested and risked the millions of dollars required to start and operate your own company.

If Xuan and Rich were to have the exact same production at HGI as they did at WMA/WFG, which paid them both approximately a half billion dollars in commissions, odds are, they would probably *double* their earnings at HGI over a similar period of time.

Likewise, if you plant your career flag with HGI for the next fifteen, twenty, thirty, or forty years, as Xuan and Rich did at WMA/WFG, you, too, will have a shot at earning one or two billion dollars in commissions in the future.

It goes without saying that we can't guarantee how much money anyone will make; all we can do is provide an opportunity where you can possibly achieve your dreams. But isn't it exciting to know that there is an opportunity that has successfully produced leaders who are making tremendous amounts of money? Of course, since this business and all others that we have ever built require lots of effort and commitment to succeed, the reality is that there will be far more people who don't make big money.

The fact is that by using our System, it's been proven that not only could I become wealthy, but other leaders like Xuan and Rich and you could too, by duplicating my wealth-building success.

CHAPTER 83

MY DREAMS CAME TRUE

THERE ARE ALL KINDS OF WORTHWHILE DREAMS, SUCH AS BEING a good person, having a good family, having a good spiritual life, and being financially independent. But as I dared to dream the *impossible* dream, a whole new way of life opened to me.

I was fortunate to be ready when the window of opportunity opened. I was able to build a business big enough to produce the kind of wealth that could make my biggest dreams a reality. The first dream was to free myself from the railroad job so I could control my own time. Achieving this allowed me to chart my own course in life and fulfill my destiny. I was able to create my own lifestyle and build a legacy for my family. From there, I continued to constantly dream bigger things than I ever thought possible, proving to myself and to all of my key leaders that if I could make my dreams come true, they could too by using our great success principles.

Along with these most important accomplishments, I lived the lifestyle of the rich and famous. Over the course of my career, I have had mansions, a world-class car collection including a variety of expensive luxury and sports vehicles, and thirteen personal jets. I have traveled the world, taken exotic vacations, relaxed on luxurious yachts. My family, teammates, and I have attended top-tier events, from Super Bowls, college football championships, and basketball Final Four games, to baseball's World Series and the Masters in golf. We've held season tickets of almost every kind. And I wasn't just a spectator; I've played golf all over the world, rubbed shoulders

with some of business's most prominent leaders, been philanthropic with my blessings, and so much more. We have filled
arenas for many of our conventions, including one we hosted
at the MGM Grand Garden Arena for 27,500 people in 1998.

Over the years, we've been entertained by and learned from
great talents at these historic events, including Tom Peters,
Muhammad Ali, Pat Riley, Stephen R. Covey, Tony Robbins,
the Simon Sinek Company, General Norman Schwarzkopf,
Joe Namath, Buzz Aldrin, the Beach Boys, the Pointer Sisters,
Huey Lewis and the News, KC and the Sunshine Band, Russell
Peters, Price Pritchett, and Paul Dietrich, just to name a few.

Norma and I built a mansion named *Le Rêve,* which, in
French, means *The Dream.* On that property we had an eigh-
teen-hole golf course, horse stables, tennis and basketball
courts, a four-acre lake, a greenhouse, a pool, a 1950s-style
diner, a bowling alley, a golf simulator, a replica of the Fox
Theater in Atlanta, and more. Our estate received recognition
in 2008 when it was featured as one of the Top 100 Homes in
Christie's Great Estates global magazine, and *Success from Home* magazine dedicated an entire issue to our company and our leaders.

I worked hard and I played hard. I worked where I played
and I played where I worked. This goes along with our type
of business. Our System allows you to not just take a vacation, but to *live* a vacation. I was not the only one achieving
my dreams. As I have shared these philosophies with my team
leaders, they were able to achieve their dreams by running
our System. I practiced this simple truth best stated by Zig
Ziglar: "You can have anything in life you want, if you will
just help enough other people get what they want."[32] I finally
learned that it's better to be a Kingmaker than to be King.
That's one of the main reasons I left ALW. I no longer felt

that there was an opportunity in that company to pull my people up to the levels that I had achieved.

Thankfully, through experience, I have learned that the real key to building solid success and happiness is to lose yourself in the service of others and become a Servant-Leader. I love the old saying sometimes attributed to Theodore Roosevelt: "No one cares how much you know until they know how much you care."

I have been blessed to enjoy an embarrassment of riches, but don't be fooled into thinking that this is what drove my success. Such creature comforts were great, but it was the chance to continue growing and to help others succeed and max out their capabilities that fueled my journey. The Scriptures tell us that we should "be in the world, but not of it" (see John 17:14). The apostle Paul said that we need to choose "a more excellent way" (1 Corinthians 12:31). And as I have already mentioned in this book, the marvelous poet Robert Frost wrote, "Two roads diverged in a wood, and I—I took the one less traveled by, and that has made all the difference."[33]

I'm committed at this phase of my life to work toward my philanthropic and charitable endeavors just as hard as I am still doing accumulating my fortune.

I'm like anyone else, so there have been several times along the way when I got a little too high and mighty or full of myself, thinking that I had everything figured out. But each time, I was humbled and brought back in line by my Heavenly Father and my sweet wife. I often think about the following story I heard as a young man by an Apostle in our church, Hugh B. Brown, in a talk entitled "God is the Gardner":

> I had purchased the farm from another who had been somewhat careless in keeping it up. I went out one

morning and found a currant bush that was at least six feet high. So, I got my pruning shears and . . . clipped it and cut it and cut it down until there was nothing left but a little clump of stumps. . . .

As I looked at this little clump of stumps, there seemed to be a tear on each one, and I said, "What's the matter, currant bush? What are you crying about?"

And I thought I heard that currant bush speak. It seemed to say, "How could you do this to me? I was making such wonderful growth. I was almost as large as the fruit tree and the shade tree, and now you have cut me down. And all in the garden will look upon me with contempt and pity. How could you do it? I thought you were the gardener here." . . .

I said, "Look, little currant bush, I *am* the gardener here, and I know what I want you to be. If I let you go the way you want to go, you will never amount to anything. But someday, when you are laden with fruit, you are going to think back and say, 'Thank you, Mr. Gardener, for cutting me down, for loving me enough to hurt me.'"[34]

You need to understand that the purpose of a currant bush is twofold: to bear fruit, and never to grow big or flower. It requires constant care and pruning to fulfill its potential.

Years later, during World War I, Hugh B. Brown was in line to get a major promotion to general in the Canadian Army. He was qualified in every way but was passed over because of his religion. He became bitter, embarrassed, and felt himself to be a failure. When he got back to his tent, he clenched his fist and shook it at heaven, saying, "How could you do this to me, God? I've done everything that I knew how to do . . . I was making such wonderful growth, and now you've cut me down. How could you do it?"

And then Hugh heard a voice. It sounded like his own voice. "I am the gardener here. I know what I want you to be. If I let you go the way you want to go, you will never amount to anything. And someday, when you are ripened in life, you are going to shout back across time and say, 'Thank you, Mr. Gardener, for cutting me down, for loving me enough to hurt me.'"[35]

I have been reminded, time after time, that I was a lot like that little currant bush, being a little too hardheaded at times to remember that God is the gardener in charge of my life. I have felt His pruning efforts shaping me in different directions than I, on my own, would have chosen to pursue. This story has always been a good governor to have in mind to keep me grounded.

And again, money wasn't my number one pursuit. I was on a great adventure, accomplishing something in my field that proved I could build and achieve at the highest levels. Having and hoarding money was never my objective. I wanted to use money and influence to help others. I desired to have possessions like jets or mansions only if they had strategic purposes and could be enjoyed by many. For most of my career, hitting earnings goals became a way to keep score among competitors and to inspire our people to achieve higher levels of prosperity and success.

Of course, my success may not be your kind of success. You have the chance to become the CEO of your own life and to pursue and achieve an unlimited number of dreams. If you apply your personal desire, focus, vision, and hard work into the right vehicle, there is a good chance your dreams will come true too.

CONQUER YOUR FUTURE

As is evident throughout this book, one of the legends I have always admired is Alexander the Great. I tell each new recruit that *to become a legend of the future, they must study the legends of the past*. You have to learn all about these people and internalize the principles they lived by and represent. Then, you must put them into action in your own life.

Here's what's important about Alexander today. He wanted the people of the future to think about him the way the people of his day thought about their great heroes in myths and legends—superhuman men such as Achilles and Ajax. That's what drove Alexander to conquer his future; he wanted to be the Achilles of his day. As he studied these great Greek heroes, he fell in love with them. Alexander saw himself as a legend, and by studying the greats of the past, he became one.

Many of us want to be great, but the key to Alexander's greatness is that he took action. And not just any action, but action fueled by both a clear goal and white-hot desire. This action led him to *conquer the known world by conquering the hearts of men*. You have to do the same in your life. You should desire to be remembered by your family, friends, coworkers, peers, and history as someone who lived life to the fullest. Be the Alexander of your day. You ultimately conquer your future by what you conquer *now*.

To do this requires that you be a dreamer. And your dream can't just be about income. Making money is fine, but you've got to want to make a difference in the world. Anyone can make money, but only the *greats* change history. People want to be significant, and I'm extending an invitation for you to be just that.

In this book I've talked about dreams, money, big houses, overrides, planes, world travel, and so forth, but I have to warn you that conquering your future isn't for the faint of heart. It's not just handed to you. Even though you may feel totally unprepared for my challenge, put your head down and take the next step, and then the next one. Inevitably, your will to win will help you develop the readiness and preparation needed for success. The word *conquer* doesn't exactly bring up visions of fun and games. It indicates that there is a fight involved. Just look at my past; there was nothing that I have that I didn't have to fight for.

You have to be incredibly mentally tough to conquer your future. As legendary NFL football coach Vince Lombardi said this about mental toughness:

"Mental toughness is essential to success.... Its qualities are sacrifice and self-denial. Also, most importantly, it is combined with a perfectly disciplined will that refuses to give in. It's a state of mind. You could call it character in action."[36]

You must declare war on everything that is standing in the way of success. I can promise you that the old saying is true: "War is hell." You have to pick up your sword and shield and get on your horse, act like a warrior, think like a general, and engage the competition. In his great book *Waging Business Warfare*, David Rogers tells us how to successfully use these Principles of War:

1. Good leadership is the prerequisite of competitive superiority.
2. Maintain your objective but be able to adjust your plans.

3. Concentrate greater strength at the decisive point. (I have found this to be the most important point of them all.)
4. Take the offensive and maintain mobility.
5. Follow the course of least resistance.
6. Achieve security by good intelligence about your competition.
7. Make certain all personnel play their part.
8. Have the element of the surprise attack.

These principles apply in our quest to conquer our futures every bit as much as they apply to actual warfare. Whatever goal you have in whatever industry you are in, be a Modern-Day Alexander by copying these greats and implementing their wisdom and strategies into your own life. The best way to motivate and inspire people is to use Alexander as a template for greatness. Because here's the thing about Alexander the Great: If he were alive today, he wouldn't be out on the battlefield trying to wage war on the world. The *world* he'd be conquering would be the business world. He wouldn't want to take over countries, but rather corporations, market share, and philanthropic charities. Remember, he would be building his giant holding company, Alexander, Inc. That's where we come in. Since Alexander isn't alive today, it's our opportunity and challenge to become the Modern-Day Alexanders of the business world. My goal is to teach those who want to learn how.

Whether it's Alexander, Napoleon, General Patton, or other great leaders, they were all decisive and persistent in their conquering pursuits. One of my favorite quotes is from Calvin Coolidge, the thirtieth president of the United States:

"Nothing in the world can take the place of PERSISTENCE.
Talent will not; nothing is more common than unsuccessful men with talent.
Genius will not; unrewarded genius is almost a proverb.
Education will not; the world is full of educated derelicts.
Persistence and Determination alone are omnipotent. The slogan "Press
On" has solved and always will solve the problems of the human race."[37]

Your charge is not to conquer other lands, but to *conquer your future.* Conquer here means that you're going to take control of your future now and be 100 percent committed to making it happen. Yes, sometimes it will be like a battle and, with sword in hand, you'll jump into the fray with the same determination that Alexander had. It will require drive and emotion, but you'll use that as fuel, instead of as an excuse to cower in the corner.

Not only have I done this, but I can share with you examples of thousands of people from all walks of life that have also done this by following my System.

I have found that all great leaders do these three things:
1. Think Strategically
2. Commit Specifically
3. Focus Constantly

It only takes a small spark to ignite a great future. All it takes is the right catalyst. Again, my promise to you is that *the rapid, relentless repetition of these simple System steps and principles will lead to the building of a more successful business life.*

I challenge you to relentlessly read and emotionalize the following affirmation:

I am ready to seize the moment. I clearly see that
my team is like Patton's Third Army—we are

precisely the right instrument, at precisely the
right moment, in exactly the right place!
I will: Plan like Alexander!
Maneuver like Napoleon!
Fight like Patton!
Build like Hubert!
I will Conquer My Future!

Now that we have prepared you to become a Modern-Day Alexander, the CEO of your own life and opportunity, it's time for you to go out and conquer your future. It's your turn. Take it!

As an African proverb reminds us, *"Every morning in Africa, an antelope wakes up. It knows it must outrun the fastest lion, or it will be killed. Every morning in Africa, a lion wakes up. It knows it must run faster than the slowest antelope or it will starve. It doesn't matter whether you're the lion or the antelope—when the sun comes up you'd better be running."*

The sun's up—are you running?

I'm calling on all of the Driven, Determined Dreamers of the world to join me on this extraordinary expedition to *conquer your future.*

ACKNOWLEDGMENTS

THIS BOOK REPRESENTS THE CULMINATION OF YEARS OF LEARNING, striving, and growing, and it would not have been possible without the contributions and support of many remarkable people.

First and foremost, I give all glory to God and my Savior, Jesus Christ, for their blessings and guidance throughout my life. Without their grace and wisdom, none of this would have been possible. They have been my constant source of strength, my ultimate inspiration, and the foundation of everything I hold dear.

A very special thank you goes to my son, Jeffrey Humphrey. Your help in crafting this book was instrumental in bringing my vision to life. Your insight, patience, and hard work are imprinted on every page.

To my family, especially my wonderful wife Norma, I am forever grateful for your unwavering love and support. You have been my rock through every triumph and challenge, and your encouragement has carried me through the most difficult times.

To my past and current associates, I offer my deepest appreciation. You have inspired, challenged, and supported me in countless ways. Our shared experiences and collective efforts have shaped both my journey and the insights shared in this book.

I also acknowledge my competitors, whose presence pushed me to strive for greater achievements and to continuously improve. The lessons learned through competition have been as essential as those learned through collaboration.

Finally, I extend my heartfelt gratitude to my publisher, Forefront Books, whose belief in this project and dedication to excellence made this book a reality and for the other professionals who helped along the way. Your expertise and guidance have been invaluable.

To everyone who has walked this journey with me, I thank you from the bottom of my heart. This book is as much yours as it is mine.

NOTES

1   Robert Frost, *The Road Not Taken and Other Poems* (New York: Dover Publications, 1993).

2   Washington Irving, "The Legend of Sleepy Hollow," in *The Sketch Book of Geoffrey Crayon, Gent.*, 1819–1820 (New York: C. S. Van Winkle, 1820), 1819-20.

3   M. Littleton, "When You Want Knowledge," *Moody Monthly*, June 1989, 29.

4   George S. Patton, *War As I Knew It* (Boston: Houghton Mifflin, 1947).

5   William Shakespeare, *Julius Caesar*, Act 4, Scene 3, in *The Complete Works of William Shakespeare* (London: Oxford University Press, 1986), 840.

6   Ken Dychtwald, *Age Wave: The Challenges and Opportunities of an Aging America* (Los Angeles: Jeremy P. Tarcher, 1989).

7   Override allows individuals to earn commissions not only on their own sales but also on the sales generated by the members of their team. https://www.getcompass.ai/glossary/overriding-commission.

8   Lewis Gordon Pugh, *Achieving the Impossible: A Fearless Leader. A Fragile Earth.* (New York: Simon & Schuster, 2010).

9   Pat Riley, *The Winner Within: A Life Plan for Team Players* (New York: Putnam Publishing Group, 1993).

10 Douglas Harper, "Enthusiasm," in *Online Etymology Dictionary*, accessed January 23, 2025, https://www.etymonline.com/word/enthusiasm.

11 Michael E. Gerber, *The E-Myth: Why Most Small Businesses Don't Work and What to Do About It* (New York: HarperBusiness, 1986).

12 John Capouya, "King Strut," *American Legacy*, December 12, 2005.

13 "Howard Cosell," *Wikipedia*, last modified January 21, 2025, https://en.wikipedia.org/wiki/Howard_Cosell.

14 Napoleon Hill, *Think and Grow Rich* (Meriden, CT: The Ralston Society, 1937).

15 Michael E. Gerber, *The E-Myth Revisited: Why Most Small Businesses Don't Work and What to Do About It* (New York: HarperBusiness, 1995).

16 Rod Serling, opening narration to *The Twilight Zone*, season 2, episode 1, aired September 30, 1960, on CBS.

17 William H. Herndon and Jesse William Weik, *Herndon's Lincoln: The True Story of a Great Life*, vol. 3 (Chicago: Belford-Clarke Co., 1889), chap. 14.

18 Eric Hoffer, *The True Believer: Thoughts on the Nature of a Mass Movement* (New York: Harper & Row, 1951).

19 William Shakespeare, *Hamlet*, edited by G. R. Hibbard (Oxford: Oxford University Press, 1987), Act 3, Scene 2, line 230. Note that the correct line from the play is "The lady doth protest too much, methinks." However, this note is referencing the speaker in the book, not the actual play.

20 J.E. McCulloch, *Home: The Savior of Civilization* (Washington, D.C.: The Southern Co-operative League, 1924), 42, quoted in David O. McKay, in Conference Report, April 1935, 116.

21 Andrew Tobias, *The Invisible Bankers: Everything the Insurance Industry Never Wanted You to Know* (New York: Simon & Schuster, 1982).

22 Michael Meyer, *The Alexander Complex* (New York: Times Books, 1989).

23 Napoleon Hill and Rosa Lee Beeland, *Think and Grow Rich* (Meriden, CT: The Ralston Society, 1937).

24 Michael Meyer, *The Alexander Complex*.

25 Don McMinn, "Stay flexible—'90% of the time we were off course'," *Don McMinn*, March 28, 2018, https://donmcminn.com/2018/03/3336/.

26 Og Mandino, *The Greatest Salesman in the World* (New York: Frederick Fell Publishers, 1968).

27 Hill, *Think and Grow Rich*.

28 Hill, *Think and Grow Rich*, 101.

29 Charlie "Tremendous" Jones, quoted in "Five Years from Now . . . ," *Tremendous Leadership*, June 17, 2018, https://tremendousleadership.com/blogs/tremendous-tracey/five-years-from-now. Note that the original source of the quote is unknown but widely attributed to Jones.

30 Michael Meyer, *The Alexander Complex*.

31 Jacob Abbott, *Alexander the Great* (Harper & Brothers, 1854), 32.

32 Zig Ziglar, quoted in "True Joy," *Ziglar Inc.*, accessed January 23, 2025, https://www.ziglar.com/quotes/true-joy/.

33 Frost, *The Road Not Taken and Other Poems*.

34 Hugh B. Brown, "God Is the Gardener," (commencement address, Brigham Young University, Provo, UT, May 31, 1968), accessed January 23, 2025, https://speeches.byu.edu/talks/hugh-b-brown/god-gardener/.

35 Brown, "God Is the Gardener."

36 Vince Lombardi Jr., *The Lombardi Rules: 26 Lessons from Vince Lombardi—The World's Greatest Coach* (McGraw Hill Professional, 2002).

37 Calvin Coolidge, quoted in *The Quotable Calvin Coolidge: Sensible Words for a New Century*, ed. Peter Hannaford (Images from the Past, 2001), 27.